MW01222983

Feed Your Kids a Better I.Q.

Feed Your Kids a Better I.Q.

Francine Prince

Harold Prince, Ph.D.

W. Foulsham & Co. Ltd.
London • New York • Toronto • Cape Town • Sydney

W. Foulsham & Company Limited
Yeovil Road, Slough, Berkshire, SL1 4JH

ISBN 0-572-01317-5
© 1987 by Harold Prince, Ph.D. and Francine Prince
Originally Published in U.S.A. by Simon and Schuster under the title of
"Feed your Kids Bright".
This anglicized edition Copyright © 1988 W. Foulsham & Co. Ltd.

Printed in Great Britain at St Edmundsbury Press
Bury St Edmunds

CONTENTS

*To
the bright kids
of today,
who will give us
the bright world
of tomorrow*

INTRODUCTION

Four Revolutions to Brightness

Quietly, with little media hype, over the last thirty years or so, four revolutions have occurred that could change the life of your kids and every kid on earth. They've happened in the canteens of schools, in the clinics and laboratories of doctors, in the research facilities of a new breed of scientist—the neurobiologists, who study the biochemistry of the brain—and in the kitchen. They've occurred independently of each other, but taken together, they tell you, for the very first time, how to bring up your kids healthy, happy, and bright with the help of the foods you feed them. Here and in the recipes on page 108 you'll find all the menus you need to do just that, and for eating for intelligence, 'eating bright'.

The menus are practical—they're created almost entirely from supermarket foods. They're familiar—the dishes are mostly healthy taste-alike and look-alikes of well-known favourites. They're time- and labour-saving—each menu, with simple adaptation, serves the whole family, even when you're pregnant or breastfeeding. They're pleasurable transitions to a new way of eating that will feed you and your spouse right while they feed your kids to brightness.

What Is Brightness?

Brightness is not simply I.Q., although that's part of it; and the right diet has raised kids' I.Q.s by as many as 35 points. Brightness is, among many subtle and splendid things, an awareness in the child of the emotional needs of others—an awareness that creates a child's affection, gentleness, helpfulness, and sense of humour. A bright child is a delight to be with.

Brightness is a friendly relationship with things, with the surrounding world and the game of hide-and-seek it plays with kids: I'm hiding things from you, come and seek them out. Brightness is curiosity, the fascination with the unknown, the delight of probing, the joy of discovery—the discovery of a world in which the child lives without fear

9

because the child knows it's understandable. Every bright child rediscovers the world so that the child can live with it, friend-with-friend.

Brightness is getting the most out of life. To find all the wondrous things life has to offer, the child must open door after door to new experiences—and that's learning. Learning is the key to making the most pleasurable selection from life's wonders—and the bright child knows this deep down. A bright child has no problems about learning. He—she—wants to learn more, faster.

A bright child is at peace and peaceful. There is no urge to win at all costs, to fight with other kids, to see life as conflict. But if success does come by effort and industry and service to others, the bright child accepts it gracefully without boasting and arrogance, and with the joy that comes with accomplishment. The bright child is a balanced child. A balanced child is a loving child. And a lovable one.

Can the right diet evoke this remarkable child? Of course not. Genes are unchangeable. Parental influence is ponderous. Schools can be a passage to the stars, but they can also be straightjackets. Peer pressure can act like a mind-altering drug. Poverty is a foe of brightness. So is affluence. Television deprives the child of the mental stimulation without which brightness cannot mature. Some social climates, moral attitudes and standards of success can stifle brightness. The road to brightness is not a smooth one. But putting your child on that road with sound nutrition can help your child get over the rough spots.

The nutrition/brightness revolution in the schools has demonstrated this. With a switch of diet, your child *can* read, your child *can* learn. The nutrition/brightness revolution in medical research has helped turn unhappy, miserable, unfit kids into happy-at-home-and-at-school winners via diet. Diet according to the neurobiologists who created the nutrition/brightness revolution in brain research, is responsible for the successful birth of the child's brain in embryo, and the astounding second birth of the brain in the newborn up to the ages of three to five. And the same diet that makes kids healthy, the women of the nutrition revolution in the kitchen have discovered, can make kids bright.

You'll learn from the breakthroughs of the pioneers who created the nutrition/brightness revolution in the kitchen, who translated the science of the nutrition/brightness revolutions into bright meals for kids and right meals for their parents. The hard science of symposia and scientific journals, of formulas and tables and charts, of laboratory analyses and computer input/output is presented here in a language as simple as your morning newspaper's. Knowing the *why* of the care of your kids is your inalienable right as a parent.

You'll learn *how* the nutrition/brightness revolutions bettered the lives of vast numbers of children throughout the world, kids who could be very much like yours. You'll meet kids with names and faces and individual personalities, who might have been sedated and institutionalised were it not for simple nutritional measures. You'll witness the ways kids, suffering from a plethora of learning disabilities from hyperactivity to symptoms of schizophrenia, have been restored to mental health, and then advanced to brightness, through nutrition.

Most importantly, you'll learn how you can help protect your child—starting even before conception—from the tragic epidemic of children's mental disorders that is sweeping Britain and America, and bring up your child bright instead. The *how* is an eating plan, presented for the first time here in this book, based on four sound principles that have emerged from the nutrition/brightness revolutions:

- Your child's brain is a biochemical machine. It's built on biochemicals. It grows on biochemicals. It works on biochemicals.
- There's only one way your child can get those biochemicals—from the right nutrients in the right amounts.
- There's only one way your child can get the right nutrients in the right amounts—from a new kind of diet; for you, from conception through pregnancy and breast-feeding, and for your child, from infancy to adolescence.
- It's a diet that generates the full quota of biochemicals your child's brain needs to develop to its peak potential for thinking, for feeling, for acting—for brightness.

This diet is our Eating Plan for Brighter Kids—the cornerstone of which is the Basic All-Family Menu Plan—a plan that is as healthful to your child's body as it is to your ciild's brain. Built on the foundations of government dietary guidelines and the recommendations of top paediatricians for the nutritional care of mother and child, it incorporates all the major findings of the four nutritional revolutions accepted by experts in nutrition.

It's a diet that's easy to get used to because it includes

familiar favourites—like burgers, chips and milk shakes—only healthful ones. It's a diet for the whole family that's easily adapted to pregnancy and breastfeeding and the changing nutrition needs of your growing kids. It's a diet that goes on from familiar favourites to exciting new taste adventures. It's a delicious, healthful diet that you can cook—the menu plans and the recipes are all here—for feeding you and your husband right while feeding your kids bright.

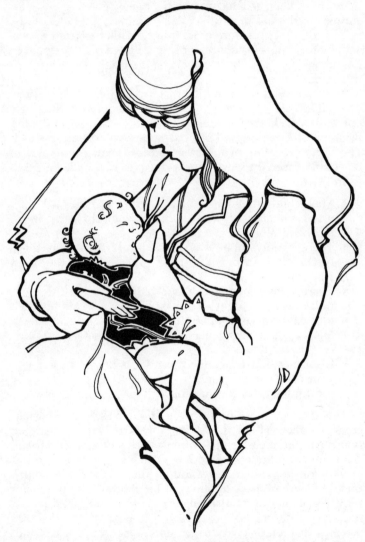

PART I

The Nutrition/ Brightness Revolution in the Schools

CHAPTER I

'EAT TO LEARN! LEARN TO EAT!'

For School Kids: Food for the Body to Expand the Mind

If your kids have learning problems, will better food solve the problem? Will eating breakfast make your school kids brighter? Will eating snacks? Can junk food be responsible for your kids' difficulties at school? Can the right kind of lunch improve school performance? How can *you* get your school kids to eat right?

Sara Sloan, as director of Food and Nutrition Programmes for US schools, was responsible for the feeding of 109 million kids over thirty-one years, found the answers.

She switched her kids from the wrong foods to the right foods, from the wrong eating habits to the right eating habits—and the results were astounding: now children could read, sit still, remember, concentrate, write, complete assignments, be quiet when quiet was called for, build a vocabulary, express themselves, stay with a subject for a long time, *learn*.

"Children were happier", says Sara Sloan. These were the kids who had been grouchy and irritable. Kids who had been depressed. Kids who had been hostile, aggressive. Kids who had acted up. Kids who had been nervous and moody. Kids who had been pint-sized Jekyll and Hydes. "These were the kids who made the classroom a combat zone", Sara Sloan says. "But now they were a delight to be with".

Fed right, the kids were healthier too. Headaches, stomach upsets, colds, allergies, vague don't-feel-well aches and pains sharply declined. So did visits to the school nurse. Tiredness, that blatant barometer of poor health (some kids were so chronically fatigued they couldn't even play), gave way to the normal high energy level of childhood.

"The right foods", Sara Sloan says, "helped open the doors to interest, curiosity, enthusiasm, imagination, motivation and the courage to try something new. "The right teachers led them through the doors".

Here's how Sara Sloan created a revolution in school kids' eating patterns for breakfast, snacks, and lunch—and how these patterns can help your kids to brightness—and how they form one of the solid foundations on which we've built our Eating Plan for Brighter Kids.

Bright Kids Eat Breakfast

In the school system of Fulton County, Georgia, there was an epidemic of 'morning dopiness'. There was no medical name for the disorder, the school doctors had no treatment for it, but the symptoms were putting stress on the teachers and disturbing the other kids. Dullness went along with restlessness, lack of interest with hostility. Sara Sloan found that many of the kids were not eating breakfast, and to her that was the explanation. "A kid whose last meal is dinner the night before", she explains, "is going about sixteen hours without food, and that kid is *hungry*. Put a hungry kid in a classroom, and all the kid's going to be interested in is when am I going to eat, not in reading, writing, and arithmetic. An empty stomach means an empty mind".

To prove her point, she introduced a nutritious morning snack into the classroom (there were no facilities for a full breakfast). Her Peanut Butter Balls are a well-balanced minimeal. She taught teachers how to make them and the teachers taught the kids. "As soon as the kids arrived at school", she says, "they mixed peanut butter with non-fat dried milk, shaped them into balls, and rolled them in crushed seeds.

The kids had fun making them. The kids loved them". Morning dopiness disappeared in many of the kids, and C's and D's began to turn into B's and A's. "Bright kids", says Sara Sloan, "eat breakfasts". Recent research reinforces the importance of breakfast for children. Children make more mistakes when tested or perform certain tasks more poorly, when breakfast is skipped.

Bright Kids Eat *Nutritious* Breakfasts

Many of the kids who ate breakfasts—"hearty breakfasts", their mothers said—also suffered from morning dopiness. "But you know what kind of breakfasts were they eating?" Sara Sloan asks. "Kids' breakfast cereals. Junk-food breakfasts. Almost all sugar, almost no nutrition. Those kids were almost as nutrition-starved as the kids who ate no breakfast, and they behaved the same way. Junk-food breakfasts are as bad as no breakfasts at all.

Bright Kids Eat Nutritious Snacks

In the early 1970s, a controversy was raging among health professionals about whether or not snacks were good for kids, with fashionable opinion deciding that they were not. But Sara Sloan had seen her morning Peanut Butter Balls work wonders for her kids, and she was on the side of snacks—the right kind of snacks.

"Kids really don't need snacks in the morning if they have a nutritious breakfast, but they do need them after school. That's the way kids are made", she says. They get ravenous after school. There's nothing wrong with afternoon snacks. What was wrong was that the kids were eating the wrong kinds of snacks".

Most snacks were junk foods. Not only the vending machines' irresistible array of sweets for kids but also brought-from-home commercial jam on processed white bread with chocolate milk. Sara Sloan was among the first to realise how badly junk-food snacks affect school performance—even though they're eaten after school.

"Sugar is in everything", she says, "and it's just terrible for kids. It give them a lift after school—a burst of energy when they need it —but then it lets them down, depresses them. They get 'sugar blues'—and that's no state to be in when you have homework to do. And the sugar kills the appetite for dinner, and they miss all that nutrition".

15

Nutritious snacks must replace junk-food snacks, Sara Sloan decided. But astounding as it is to the health-oriented parents of today, in the early seventies there was not a single cookbook on junk-free snacks for kids, no set of guidelines, not even a list of suggestions. It wouldn't be until 1979 that the U.S. Department of Agriculture, as part of its observance of the International Year of the Child, would put its stamp of approval on groups of foods for kids from which sugar-free, junk-free snacks could be selected.

Sara Sloan was the pioneer creator of nutritious snacks for kids. Her goal was snacks of high-energy. nutrient-rich ingredients that provide kids with the midafternoon lift they need—the natural lift that never lets them down, the kind that comes with good nutrition. That's the type of snacks we've built into our Eating Plan for Brighter Kids. But, unlike most nutritious snacks, they're easily sold to kids; some actually look alike and taste like the junk-food snacks today's kids have grown to love.

Bright Kids Don't Eat Junk Foods for Lunch

In 1951, when Sara Sloan started her career as a school nutritionist, there were few problem kids, she says. "We had some backward kids and some disturbed kids, but they were the exceptions. And I think this was true of most school systems of that time".

Aware of contrasting current statistics that characterize one out of five school kids as having some type of learning disability, she sees the distressing shift in children's eating patterns since the 1950s as a root cause. "It's hard to believe", she says, "that it's only in the last thirty-five years or so that processed foods have largely replaced natural foods".

She recalls that up to the early 1950s, natural foods were the normal way of eating, and that's the way she fed her kids in the schools. "We had a nutritional paradise", she says, "but in the rush and push to meet financial requirements, we lost it". School canteens serving natural foods became fast-food school cafeterias. "When I joined the school system", she says, "no-one even dreamed that they would ever see junk food served in a school, but here it was: burgers, fries, shakes, foods with preservatives, artificial colours and flavours, lots of sugar and salt. Even salads were premixed. Chemicals were supposed to keep them fresh. But they didn't".

The effects on the kids were heartbreaking, she says. "We

had vandalism. We had rowdiness. We had disciplinary problems, usually after lunch. We never, never, had those things happen before, Marks fell, so did reading scores. There were more cases of kids who couldn't stop talking, and kids who threw temper tantrums. There· were too many depressed kids and kids suffering from chronic fatigue. More kids were visiting the nurse. There were more absentees because of sickness. Teachers said kids just didn't seem to be as healthy as they have been".

Sara Sloan's observations have been corroborated by a 1983 study conducted by Dr. Michael Colgan, a leading nutrition scientist. Coincident with the junk-food invasion which began in the early 1950s and occupied most schools by 1960, he wrote, "there has been a huge rise in the number of children with brain damage, hyperactivity, or learning disability. A study at the University of California suggests that the problem has doubled since the 1960s".

How You Can Get Your Kids to Switch to Healthful Foods

"You can lead kids to the table", mothers told Sara Sloan, "but you can't make them eat". So Sara Sloan devised several methods that worked for her multimillions of kids, and could work for your kids, too.

The simplest one, and one of the best for getting kids to try something new, was putting up this sign over healthful dishes on the canteen counter: For Adults Only. "You couldn't keep the kids away from them", she says. It's a cute idea for starters, but over the long haul it's likely to wear thin, particularly if the kids don't like what they taste. Her other ideas have more lasting impact.

Discovering that kids will eat anything they make themselves, she taught them how to cook. "What they cooked themselves, no matter how awful it turned out the first time, and how messy they got themselves and everything else— they loved it", she says. "cooking comes naturally to children of both sexes, if you just give them a chance and encourage them".

We think this is a great idea; every kid should learn how to cook—the bright way. That's why some of the recipes in this book are so easy that your kids can make them under your supervision.

Let your kids learn by watching you cook and helping you cook. Sara Sloan also recommends that kids grow some of their own food. "Kids love to see things grow", she says, "particularly if they make them grow". She suggests vegetable gardens if you live in the suburbs or the country; or, if you live in a city, sprouts grown in a jar. Sprouts are pretty messy to grow, but they grow fast, and they hold the younger kids' interest. "Kids who would never look at a vegetable or a sprout", Sara Sloan says, "eat them with as much relish as if they were Big Macs—when they grow them themselves.

"But in the final analysis it's the example you set that will put your kids on the right eating track or the wrong one", she warns. "If you feed your kids fruit for dessert while you and your husband gorge on ice cream, your kids will want ice cream, too. You have to set an example. You have to be a role model. Good nutrition is more caught than taught".

That's another reason our Eating Plan for Brighter Kids is an eating plan for the whole family, as delicious for you as it is for your kids, making your new role as your kids' teacher on eating for health and brightness easy to play.

A Junk Food-Free Diet Means Brighter Kids

Sara Sloan's Junk Food-Free diet works well—so well that thirteen- and fourteen-year-olds in her Fulton County school system at one time routinely dramatized its success with this mini-experiment: white rats were the subjects because, as one student explained, "rats react to food much the same as humans but in a much shorter time". There were six animals in the experiment, and each was given a pet name. At the start, all were bright and healthy as well-cared-for laboratory rats usually are.

Elmer and Lulu were fed only the kinds of snacks most kids ate: sweets, desserts, potato crisps, and soft drinks. They become dopey, nervous, and irritable. Dan's and Little Ann's menus were composed exclusively of hamburgers, fried potatoes and soft drinks—the kind of food most kids were served at lunch in school cafeterias nationwide. This pair became fat, apathetic, and lost their mental alertness. All four of the rats also fell ill. Their coats degenerated into raggedness, and their tails disrupted into scales and unsightly discolorations.

On the other hand, Rufus and Priscilla were fed nothing but the Sara Sloan diet. They remained as clever and happy and full of vigour as they had been when the experiment began. Maybe a little more so.

The experiment ended happily for all the rats. When the rats on the junk-food diets were switched to the better diet, they recovered completely, and the kids couldn't tell them apart.

PART II

The Nutrition/ Brightness Revolution in Medical Research

CHAPTER 2

SALICYLATES AND ADDITIVES

Foods That Could Make Your Kids Hyperactive

In the 1950s a strange new malady, now claiming some 5 million victims, began to rampage among children everywhere—hyperactivity.

The hyperactive child can't be still, not for more than seconds. With an attention span shorter than it takes to read a line of type, he can't learn. He goes on unstoppable verbal marathons. Irritated by almost anything, he responds with aggression. He's a real Dennis the Menace. No classroom can withstand his violent disruptiveness. For reasons no-one yet can fathom, there are more 'he's' among hyperactives than 'she's'.

Not every hyperactive is a one-kid reign of terror. But even the mildest form of hyperactivity can be heartbreaking to parents and teachers, and life-shattering to a child. Your child is probably hyperactive if you find yourself checking off every symptom listed on the chart "Is Your Child Hyperactive?" (opposite).

But even if the answer is "no", your child could become hyperactive when certain amounts of the foods that are in the diet of virtually every kid are consumed. Dr. Ben F. Feingold, the California paediatrician who made this path-breaking discovery, classifies the hyperactive-inducing foods into two types: foods containing salicylates (naturally occurring aspirin-like chemicals in foods), and foods containing additives.

Protecting Your Kids from Salicylates

Dr. Feingold's discovery linking salicylate-containing foods to hyperactivity was, like so many other great scientific discoveries, serendipitous. He had observed that some hyperactive kids on aspirin were no longer hyperactive when taken off the drug. Aspirin is a member of a class of chemicals called the salicylates.

But some kids who had never taken aspirin in their lives were also hyperactive. How to explain? With a brilliant flash of insight, Dr. Feingold searched for salicylates that occurred naturally *in foods*. He found them. When he removed the salicylate-containing foods from some hyperactive's diets, the disorder disappeared.

There is a list of salicylate-containing foods on page 22. If, after eating any of them, your kids become hyperactive, you can follow Dr. Feingold's therapy, and eliminate them from their diet. Keeping these foods off their diet, even if your kids don't show symptoms of hyperactivity, can prevent salicylate-induced hyperactivity from ever striking.

Is Your Child Hyperactive?

A tick in each box indicates the classic syndrome of hyperactivity. Any child may become hyperactive after consumption of trigger amounts of foods containing salicylates or additives.

☐ Can't sit still
☐ Can't keep quiet
☐ Learning difficulties
☐ Intensely aggressive
☐ Impertinent
☐ Disrespectful
☐ Short attention span

☐ Uncontrollable
☐ Sleeping problems
☐ Poor motor coordination
☐ Flares up easily
☐ Disrupts household, playground, classroom

21

Until recently, elimination of salicylates was the only way to prevent and cure salicylate-induced hyperactivity. Now there's a new way based on discoveries, made by dozens of independent medical investigators, that explain how salicylates work in the brain to induce hyperactivity. What these investigators learned is this: salicylates sharply reduce the amounts of vitamin C in children's brains, as well as vitamins of the B-complex and the minerals calcium, potassium, and iron. Deprivation of *any* nutrients may result in hyperactivity, and salicylates cause deprivation of *all* of them.

To offset the effects of salicylate-containing foods *without removing them from your kids' diet*, today's nutrition scientists recommend a diet with the right amounts of vitamins and minerals to compensate for the loss of those nutrients due to salicylates.

Do Your Kids Exhibit Hyperactivity Symptoms After Eating Any of These Foods?

If they do, the hyperactivity is induced by aspirin-like substances, called salicylates, in the foods. You can then remove these foods from your kids' meals, or you can switch your kids to our Eating Plan for Brighter Kids. It protects against salicylates, and lets your kids enjoy these tasty and nutritious foods.

Fruits
☐ Apples
☐ Apricots
☐ Blackberries
☐ Cherries
☐ Currants
☐ Gooseberries
☐ Grapes
☐ Nectarines
☐ Oranges
☐ Peaches
☐ Plums
☐ Prunes
☐ Raisins
☐ Raspberries
☐ Strawberries

Vegetables
☐ Cucumbers, cucumber pickles
☐ Tomatoes, tomato products

Protecting Your Kids Against Additives

Dr. Feingold found that in some of his patients the elimination of salicylate-rich foods did not remedy hyperactivity. Could there be other substances in foods that produced the disorder? He put two and two together. Before the 1950s hyperactivity was virtually unknown. But during the 1950s the processed-food industry expanded enormously. Throughout the nation, natural foods were replaced with foods containing additives—chemical colourings, flavourings, preservatives, stimulants, and processing ingredients. Could additives cause hyperactivity?

The first indication that they could came, surprisingly, from an adult patient. Before coming to Dr. Feingold, she had undergone psychotherapy for years with no success. When Dr. Feingold switched the psychotherapeutic drug she was on to one containing no artificial colouring, she was suddenly cured. If an abnormal emotional/behavioural problem in an adult could be caused by an additive, surely, Dr. Feingold reasoned, it was possible for additives to cause hyperactivity in a child.

Dr. Feingold examined the diets of hyperactive kids who were not cured by salicylate-food elimination. All of those diets contained additives. When Dr. Feingold switched the diets back to natural foods (as Sara Sloan was doing about the same time for her kids, and with similar results), hyperactivity changed back to normality.

But the parents who cut down, without entirely eliminating hyperactivity-inducing foods in their kids' diets, found no off switch. The reason, Dr. Feingold discovered after years of persistent investigation, is that the substances in food that activate hyperactivity are effective in extremely small quantities.

"I remain stunned", he wrote after he made that discovery, "by the infinitesimal amounts of activator [needed] . . . stunned that any substance of 50 trillionth of a gram could react in the human [brain]". To defeat hyperactivity, he told parents, foods that induce it must be banned *entirely*. A list of Dr. Feingold's hyperactivity-inducing foods appears on pages 25 and 26.

But just a cursory glance at Dr. Feingold's forbidden list is enough to frighten off most mothers. It eliminates virtually all packaged, canned, frozen, and fast foods; and it puts all but the fresh food departments of the supermarket out of bounds. The strains of extended kitchen-and-shopping time and getting the kids accustomed to new tastes, on top of the burden of preparing one meal for the hyperactive kids and another for the rest of the family, makes acceptance of Dr. Feingold spartan regime difficult to impossible.

That's one reason doctors, realizing that a non-additive diet is sooner or later rejected, prescribe drugs for hyperactive kids. But they don't work. Hyperactive kids are treated mainly with members of a family of drugs called central nervous system stimulants. Paradoxically, these drugs do not stimulate hyperactive kids as they do other kids and adults, but rather calm them down. But abnormally so—a full pendulum swing.

Doctors also prescribe members of the phenothiazine family of sedative drugs for some cases of hyperactivity. Originally formulated for use in treatment of psychiatric disorders characterised by psychotic agitation, aggressiveness, and explosive, intense excitability, these drugs are claimed by the manufacturers to be effective on hyperactive kids when used over a short period.

But the side effects can be devastating. Some of them actually accomplish the reverse of what the drugs are supposed to do, producing such symptoms as restlessness, excitement, trembling, shaking hands and fingers, jerky movements of hands and neck, involuntary tongue and mouth movements, and fast heartbeat. Intense drowsiness and sharp decline of mental alertness may result as well, sometimes accompanied by light-headedness, dizziness, and fainting.

"Drugs resolve no . . . problems", writes Dr. Allen Cott, referring to their use in the treatment of hyperactivity and other learning disorders. *"They only disguise symptoms temporarily* (emphasis his)". He points out that drug therapy for children with learning problems including hyperactivity has been banned in Sweden and Japan, commenting that it's "certainly a wise measure".

Additive-Containing Foods That Can Trigger Hyperactivity

Each child has an individual trigger level at which certain amounts of additives can induce hyperactivity. Trigger levels are so low in some children that they're reached by infinitesimal amounts of additives. The best way to prevent your children from reaching these levels is to strike all additive-containing foods from their diet.

The additive-containing foods in this list, compiled by Dr. Ben F. Feingold, are included in our 181 Worst Foods for Your Kids' Brains in Chapter 10. Many are replaced in our Eating Plan for Brighter Kids with healthful non-additive taste-alikes.

Breakfast Cereals

All with artificial colours or flavours
All instant breakfast preparations

Baked Goods

All manufactured baked goods, fresh and frozen, including cakes, biscuits, pastry, sweet rolls, pies, doughnuts, and breads
All packaged baking mixes

Luncheon Meats

All packaged meats, including garlic sausage, salami, frankfurters, sausages, meat loaf, bacon, ham, and pork

Poultry

All barbecued and self-basting poultry
All prepared stuffing

Fish

All crab sticks
All artificially dyed or flavoured frozen fillets

Desserts

All ice creams, sorbets, and ices
All gelatine and junket desserts
All puddings
All dessert mixes
All flavoured yoghurts

Sweets

All manufactured sweets

Beverages

All instant breakfast drinks
All quick-mix powdered drinks
Tea, coffee, and chocolate milk
Soft drinks, including diet drinks

Other Items

All mint-flavoured items
All mustards and ketchups
Soy sauces that are artificially flavoured or coloured,
and chilli sauces
Artificially coloured butter and margarine
Cider and wine vinegar
Cloves

CHAPTER 3

'CEREBRAL ALLERGENS'

Foods That Could Make Your Kids Slow Learners

The 1950s saw the epidemic rise of learning disabilities, not yet abated, of which hyperactivity is one major cause. There's another, the opposite of hyperactivity: the slow-learning syndrome. Its mental symptoms are fatigue, drowsiness, depression, anxiety, and a feeling of tension, always accompanied by slow learning.

Puzzled by this syndrome—which was not then effectively treated (as it still is not today) by therapeutic drugs, psychiatry, or counselling—paediatrician Dr. William G. Crook, following Dr. Feingold's lead, looked for the foods that cause it.

After about 20 years of clinical research, which incorporated the results of ouher investigators, he found them. In 1973, he introduced to an astonished general public a new class of foods that could affect kids adversely—cerebral allergens. These are so called, he said, because they have an allergic effect on kids' brains.

Are Your Kids Slow Learners Because of Cerebral Allergens?

Dr. Crook discovered a simple way for you to find out if cerebral allergens are implicated. Cerebral allergens, he learned, are likely to be the cause of slow learning when the complete slow-learning syndrome is accompanied by at least a few of the follwing physical symptoms:

Physical Symptoms That May Accompany the Slow-Learning Syndrome

- ☐ Paleness
- ☐ Feeling under par
- ☐ Circles or bags under eyes
- ☐ Stuffy nose
- ☐ Sinus complaints
- ☐ Excessive sneezing
- ☐ Stomach aches
- ☐ Muscle pains
- ☐ Itching
- ☐ Rashes
- ☐ Bedwetting or other urinary problems
- ☐ Headaches
- ☐ Puffiness or bloating
- ☐ Coughing or wheezing
- ☐ Chest discomfort

If a kid of yours *is* a slow learner because of cerebral allergens, then one or more of the following foods may be responsible:

The Slow-Learning Foods

- ☐ Beans, particularly soya beans
- ☐ Breads and other baked goods
- ☐ Breakfast cereals
- ☐ Corn and corn products such as corn oil and corn chips
- ☐ Grapefruit
- ☐ Lemons
- ☐ Lentils
- ☐ Limes
- ☐ Malted milks
- ☐ Oranges
- ☐ Pancakes
- ☐ Peanuts
- ☐ Peas
- ☐ Potatoes
- ☐ Soy Sauce
- ☐ Stuffings
- ☐ Tofu (bean curd)
- ☐ Waffles
- ☐ Wheatgerm

But *which* of these cerebral allergens affects *your* child? Dr. Crook has discovered that a cerebral allergen that triggers the total slow-learning syndrome (physical and mental symptoms) in one child, need not be the one that triggers it in another. To pinpoint the specific cerebral allergens affecting your child, Dr. Crook pioneered a method now recommended, with variations, by many physicians:

- You feed your child an 'elimination diet' that leaves out a single possible cerebral allergen for seven to eight days.

- Should the symptoms of the total slow-learning syndrome improve for two days, then you've found a 'suspect food'.

- You then return the suspect food to your child's diet; if after about a week all the symptoms return in full strength, you know the suspect food is a 'guilty food'—a cerebral allergen.

- The food is then permanently eliminated from the child's diet.

- When it is, or when several cerebral allergens discovered in the same way are eliminated, your slow-learning child's life can be turned around.

But Dr. Crook's cerebral allergen treatment, as sound and effective as it is, has several partial drawbacks. Most elimination diet searches for specific cerebral allergens are not as simple as they appear to be. Many foods may have to undergo the elimination test before a guilty food is found. Often many guilty foods are involved, and then the search becomes complex and prolonged, and must be undertaken under medical supervision. Cost, time, and tension mount.

Besides, mothers found—as other mothers had found when their kids had been put on Dr. Feingold's additive-free diet—that a special diet for one or more kids in the family creates problems. Preparing two meals, one for the afflicted kids, and the other for the rest of the family, is a gruelling chore. Kids resent having to give up foods they've been accustomed to. Parents worry about their kids missing the nutrients in the banned foods.

Parents told Dr. Crook that the elimination diet is worth all the money, time and emotional costs involved, but they wished there was an easier way. There is—now. It is based on the most recent discoveries of medical allergy specialists and medical nutrition scientists concerning Dr. Crook's cerebral allergens.

The New Way to Feed Slow-Learning Kids to Brightness

The first discovery is that cerebral allergens are not allergens. To Dr. Crook, an allergy is "a hypersensitivity to a specific substance which, in similar quantity, does not bother other people". That 'specific substance' is an allergen. Not necessarily so, respond medical allergy specialists. For a substance to be an allergen, it must react with antibodies (proteins normally necessary to the body's defence against disease) to create a harmful reaction—all allergic reaction.

Only a laboratory test, these specialists assert, can determine whether a substance reacts harmfully with antibodies, and is indeed an allergen. They found that Dr. Crook's list of cerebral allergens, the ones that passed his elimination test could not pass their laboratory test. The foods that Dr. Crook had identified as causing slow-learning in kids were not allergens.

Actually, Dr. Crook didn't know what they were. He had adopted the term *allergen* because when he began his research allergy was a medical fad, and doctors were diagnosing symptoms they didn't understand as an 'allergen' (as now they're diagnosing them as a 'virus'). But of one thing Dr. Crook was certain: the foods he had identified *did* cause the total slow-learning syndrome.

Today's medical nutrition scientists agree, but their research points to a new explanation of how these foods act on kids' brains. What appears to happen is this: the cerebral allergens diminish the brain's supply of certain vitamins and minerals below the levels that prevent the total slow-learning syndrome. Those levels are different for every child, which explains why some kids are affected and some are not.

The minerals include calcium, copper, iron, magnesium, phosphorus, zinc, selenium and chromium. Among the vitamins are vitamin C, and those of the B-complex, especially B_6 and pantothenic acid. There is good evidence to suggest that many of those nutrients help protect as well against allergens other than cerebral ones.

Nutrition scientists point out that when the quantities of the vitamins and minerals lost to kids' brains by the action of the cerebral allergens are replenished by a diet high in those nutrients, the cerebral allergens need not be removed from kids' diet. One study demonstrated that on this type of diet, I.Q.'s rapidly soared up to 35 points; and in another study, reading scores improved markedly.

The chances are you'll find it difficult to create a diet with just the right amounts of the vitamins and minerals your kids need to fight cerebral allergens. Too little would be ineffective; too much would be dangerous. Our Eating Plan for Brighter Kids removes that difficulty for you by providing the optimal amounts of vitamins and minerals to help protect your child against the slow-learning syndrome.

CHAPTER 4

SUGAR

Foods That Could Turn Your Kids into Jekyll and Hydes

The world's most popular sweetener is pure, white, crystalline sucrose—sugar. Anxious mothers complain to doctors that their normal kids 'climb the walls' after birthdays, holidays, and party treats—that is, after they've gorged themselves with sugar-packed sweets, cakes, and ice creams. Doctors' records are replete with cases of well-behaved kids who suddenly explode with anger, go into temper tantrums, and flare into irrational outbursts following sugar-filled meals. A study of the American Institute of Biosocial Research, Jacksonville Beach, Florida, conducted by Alexander C. Schauss, linked the onset of learning disabilities to a high-sugar diet, and found that when the diet was continued, nine out of ten of the learning-disabled kids developed into juvenile delinquents.

When Dr. Stephen J. Schoenthaler, coordinator of the criminal justice research programme at California State University, switched juvenile delinquents in 17 correction institutions and 803 schools to a low- or no-sugar diet, he found he could "reduce by half antisocial behaviour like assault, theft and insubordination". What all this evidence, and much more like it, demonstrates dramatically is at bottom a simple fact: many kids on high-sugar meals are Hydes, and on low-sugar meals become Jekylls and vice versa.

Can You Keep Sugar in Your Kids' Diet?

No. These are the reasons: sugar, because it stimulates the flow of insulin, depresses the amount of glucose in your child's bloodstream. Not enough glucose, the brain's source of energy, is carried to the brain. Among the many symptoms of low glucose are: irritability, loss of concentration and attention, faltering memory, depression, anxiety, light-headedness, dizziness, insomnia, fatigue, and exhaustion.

Even in the mildest cases of this sugar-induced disorder Dr. Allan Cott observes, "The brain function . . . is impaired. Even if [a child] does not suffer from a learning disability, he will not learn as well as he should". The simplest, safest, and the only effective way to prevent or reverse sugar-induced low-glucose symptoms is to eliminate dietary sugar.

Sugar leads to physical disorders as well. Professor John Yudkin, the leading British pioneer among medical nutritional scientists, in his aptly entitled book *Pure, White and Deadly*, associated the sweetener with an astonishing spectrum of diseases. They include obesity, diabetes, gout, atherosclerosis, heart attack, enlargement of the liver, kidney damage, chronic indigestion, gastric and duodenal ulcers, and dental decay.

There's no way to prevent sugar's contribution to an onset of these diseases except by removing the sweetener from your kids' menus. Sugar also undernourishes your children even though it seems that they're well fed. Here's what happens: if your child's diet is like the diet of most children, it's 50 per cent sugar in terms of total calories. Sugar is an 'empty calorie' food—a food that contributes calories (energy) but no, or virtually no, vitamins and minerals. Subtract 50 per cent of sugar's empty calories from the, say, 1200 calories each of your children consumes daily, and that leaves 600 calories a day of nutritious foods (provided all the non-sugar foods are nutritious, which they're probably not). That's undernourishment.

In addition to curtailing growth and weakening your child's resistance to disease, undernourishment produces these symptoms: lack of concentration, memory loss, irritability, depression, and inability to think clearly.

Can You Use Sugar Substitutes?

Yes and no. Many sugar substitutes are also empty-calorie foods; other substitutes are disqualified for other health reasons. But some substitutes are excellent. Let the list on pages 33 to 35 be your guide. It was ours when we prepared our Eating Plan for Brighter Kids.

But aren't kids born with a taste for sugar—real sugar? If that's so, then kids have been deprived for all but a few of the many long years that the human race has been on earth. Sugar did not become a popular food until more than a hundred years ago when it was introduced in England as a stimulant (in tea, another stimulant) to fight off exhaustion among the men, women, *and* children who toiled for twelve to sixteen hours without breaks in Britain's mills and factories. The use of sugar then spread throughout the industrial West, and then to the world.

Nowhere in the scientific literature is there any evidence that kids are born with a taste for sugar. Dr. Allan Cott states flatly, "No baby is born with a sweet tooth. A child will not clamour for more sweet foods, unless the child has been fed sweet foods. The taste [for sugar] is acquired". *Easily* acquired. But, as every health-conscious mother knows, hard to break. Until now.

How To Break Your Kids' Sugar Habit

It's smart to start by banning sugar from your kitchen—out of sight is out of mouth—but the more than half a pound of sugar daily (and rising) that average adults consume doesn't come from the sugar they spoon into their tea or coffee, but from the sugar hidden in virtually all junk foods. Sugar is insidiously omnipresent in soft drinks; chocolates; pies; biscuits; puddings; jams and jellies; all yoghurts except plain; baking mixes; breads; breakfasts cereals; ketchup and other condiments; and even in canned, frozen, and packed meats, poultry, fish, and vegetables.

A Parent's Guide to Sugar Substitutes

Substitute	Guideline	Comments
Aspartame	Do not use.	
Beet sugar (raw, unrefined; 96 per cent SUCROSE)	Do not use.	Empty-calorie food.
Blackstrap molasses (96 per cent SUCROSE)	Do not use.	Empty-calorie food.
Brown sugar (sucrose plus a small quantity of molasses)	Do not use.	Empty-calorie food.
Cane sugar (raw, unrefined; 96 per cent SUCROSE)	Do not use.	Empty-calorie food.
Carrot juice	Okay to use, but see comments.	Excessive use may result in liver damage in susceptible kids (and adults).
Coconut	Use sparingly.	Good supply of nutrients, but high in saturated fat, which can be harmful in excess.
Corn syrup (an invert type of sugar; see INVERT SUGAR)	Do not use.	Empty-calorie food.
Date powder (crushed dried dates)	Okay to use.	Good supply of nutrients.
Date sugar (same as DATE POWDER)	Okay to use.	Good supply of nutrients.
Dextrins (chemical relatives of DEXTROSE)	Do not use.	Empty-calorie food.
Dextrose (a form of GLUCOSE)	Do not use.	Empty-calorie food.
Dried fruits (raisins, dates, apples, bananas, etc.)	Okay to use.	Good supply of nutrients.
Fructose (refined fruit sugar)	Do not use.	Empty-calorie food.

A Parent's Guide to Sugar Substitutes (cont.)

Substitute	Guideline	Comments
Fruit (raw or cooked without sugar)	Okay to use.	Good supply of nutrients.
Fruit juices (fresh or frozen concentrates)	Okay to use.	Good supply of nutrients; fresh is better.
Fruits pastes (no sugar or salt added)	Okay to use.	Good supply of nutrients.
Glucose (a principal constituent of SUCROSE)	Do not use.	Empty-calorie food.
Herbs (sweet: such as aniseed, marjoram, oregano, rosemary, sweet basil, and tarragon)	Okay to use.	Good supply of nutrients.
Honey (raw, unfiltered, uncooked)	Okay to use, but see comments.	Good supply of nutrients, *but do not use* for children under the age of 1 (raw honey has been implicated in infant deaths), and *do not use* if honey has been made from nectar of the following plants: azalea, mountain laurel, yellow jasmine and some rhododendrons. These honeys may be toxic.
Honey (processed)	Do not use.	Much of the nutrient value has been destroyed in processing.
Invert sugar (commercial name for hydrolised sucrose—a mixture of roughly equal amounts of FRUCTOSE and GLUCOSE)	Do not use.	Empty-calorie food.
Mannitol (a sugar-like substance)	Do not use.	Empty-calorie food.
Maple syrup (100 per cent pure, untreated)	Use sparingly, but see comments.	Low nutrient value, due to extraction process.

Food	Recommendation	Comments
Maple syrup (commercial, a mixture of CORN and SUCROSE SYRUPS plus artificial colouring, with little MAPLE SYRUP)	Do not use.	Empty-calorie food, worsened by artificial colouring.
Nut pastes (no sugar or salt added)	Okay to use.	Good supply of nutrients.
NutraSweet (essential ingredient is ASPARTAME)	Do not use.	
Nuts (raw)	Okay to use.	Good supply of nutrients.
Pancake syrups (see MAPLE SYRUP, commercial)	Do not use.	See MAPLE SYRUP, commercial.
Raw sugar (96 per cent SUCROSE with a small amount of molasses)	Do not use.	Empty-calorie food.
Saccharin	Do not use.	Possible carcinogen.
Sorbitol (a sugar-like substance)	Do not use.	Empty-calorie food.
Spices such as allspice, cinnamon, coriander, ginger, mace, and mild paprika	Okay to use.	Good supply of nutrients.
Sugar Cane	Okay to use.	Good supply of nutrients.
Turbinado sugar (96 per cent SUCROSE with a small amount of molasses)	Okay to use.	Empty-calorie food.
Xylitol (a sugar-like substance)	Do not use.	Empty-calorie food.

The New 'Super-Sweeteners': Thaumatin, derived from the West African kafemfe bush, is the sweetest substance known to science—100,000 times sweeter than sugar. Monellin, which comes from the serendipity berry of another African bush, is almost as sweet. Little is known as yet about their effects on humans. Levo-O-Cal, a 'left-handed' version of sucrose, has no nutritive value at all, not even caloric value, because it cannot be metabolized by the body. None of these new super-sweeteners is yet available commercially.

Shockingly, sugar in kids' diets is even higher than in adults'—25 per cent. The blame for that rests with TV-advertised 'kids' foods'—breakfast cereals, soft drinks, snacks, desserts, frozen dinners, and fast food—all junk foods glutted with sugar. So breaking the sugar habit really means breaking the junk-food habit. That's why we've created *healthful* 'junk-food clones'—especially desserts and snacks—to replace sugar-heavy junk foods.

There are two kinds of our healthful junk foods, both deliciously sweetened with sugar-free sweeteners. One does not contain a single grain of sugar. The other contains negligible amounts of sugar. (There's no harm done by a few empty calories because the nutrient loss is made up on our high vitamin/mineral diet.) The slightly sugared junk foods help your kids make the transition to sugar-free junk foods in this way: children may not take to the taste of sugar-free clones at once; there *is* a taste difference. But the difference is not appreciable, and after a while when you introduce the sugar-free junk-food clones, your children won't taste too much difference, and will get used to them easily and enjoyably. Your kids will have acquired a new taste. Then you can drop the slightly sugared junk foods—and all real junk foods and all sugar—from your children's menus forever.

And from yours and your husband's, too, when you make the same transition. Sugar is equally bad for adults—bringing on sugar blues, threatening health with nutrition scientist Professor Yudkin's long catalogue of sugar-induced diseases, and playing havoc with hopes of slimness. Yet when you and the rest of the family switch over to non-sugar foods our healthful junk-food way, your sweet tooth will be as satisfied as it was before. This is a sweet way to break the sugar habit. You'll find a list of our healthful 'junk-food clones' in Chapter 12.

CHAPTER 5

ANTI-VITAMIN, ANTI-MINERAL FOODS

Foods That Could Dull Your Kids' Brains

Case History: Sandy, aged 10
Major Symptom: Impaired sense perceptions
Diagnosis: Pre-clinical pellagra (a skin disease)
Possible Cause: Breakfast cereals, particularly of the muesli type; corn and most corn products; seeds; vegetable greens

A pre-clinical disorder is characterized by preliminary symptoms of a disease. Pre-clinical pellagra is a disorder that affects your kids' brains. A little more than a decade ago, although kids had begun to suffer from it nationwide since the 1950s, it was not a disorder recognized by the medical profession. As a matter of fact, up to that time, the nation's doctors did not believe that such a thing as a pre-clinical disorder existed.

But once pre-clinical pellagra was discovered by the paediatrician Dr. Glen Green in the course of his treatment of Sandy, medical nutrition scientists rapidly identified several dozen more pre-clinical disorders. They all have this in common: the diseases they precede so severely impair the brain's function, that brightness is blacked out by depression or even dementia. The pre-clinical disorder, less severe, dulls kids' brains.

To Dr. Green, Sandy was exhibiting preliminary symptoms—pre-clinical symptoms—of that disease. The disease is pellagra, and it's caused by the depletion of vitamin B_3 (niacin) in kids' brains. Dr. Green started immediate treatment with vitamin B_3 supplements in quantities considerably exceeding the RDA (Recommended Dietary Allowance).

On the lookout for pre-clinical pellagra among his patients, Dr. Green found that one out of ten children was afflicted by it. Large over-RDA doses of vitamin B_3 were the cure; and when a child had been afflicted only a short time before treatment began, it was a fast cure, restoring the child to health in a few days, and sometimes overnight. RDAs are Recommended Dietary Allowances, calculated by the Food and Nutrition Board, the National Academy of Sciences National Research Council to prevent the onset in most people of nutrition-deprivation diseases, such as pellagra. These allowances are often not sufficient, however, to ward off pre-clinical symptoms of those diseases in many kids and adults.

The allowances of nutrients necessary to do that are called ODAs, Optimal Dietary Allowances. It was Dr. Green's success with over-RDA dosages of vitamin B_3 that prompted medical nutrition scientists to establish ODAs for all vitamins and minerals. ODAs are essential to help protect against pre-clinical symptoms; that's why your kids get their full ODAs of vitamin B_3, and all other vitamins and minerals, on our Eating Plan for Brighter Kids.

There are several reasons for the amount of vitamin or mineral in the brain to fall below its ODA level. But when the deficiency appears suddenly in well-nourished kids—as it did in Sandy's case—medical nutrition scientists look for special kinds of foods newly added to the kids' diet. These are foods the diminish the quantities of certain vitamins and minerals in the brain—the anti-vitamin, anti-mineral foods.

Records of nutrition scientists show that as the diet has changed over the last decade or so, the following anti-vitamin-B_3 foods have made abrupt debuts in the diet of thousands of children: some 'health foods': seeds, vegetable greens, and raw grains, particularly muesli-type breakfast cereals. Mexican foods that are based on corn, including tacos, tortillas, enchilladas, tostadas, and tamales. (Corn may not be a direct vitamin B_3 antagonist, but it is low in that vitamin as well as in the amino acid tryptophan from which the body manufactures it. The result of a diet mainly of corn or most corn products is vitamin-B_3 deprivation. Corn oil, though, is not an anti-vitamin-B_3 food).

Successful treatment of pre-clinical pellagra, from Dr. Green onwards, did not require the removal of the offending but otherwise nutritious foods from the diet. Rather, the level of vitamin B_3 in kids' brains were brought up to ODA level, and kept there through supplementation. Supplementation cannot be discontinued, because once it is, the pre-clinical symptoms return, often with greater intensity than before. This was discovered in another classic case.

Case History: Fran, aged 13
Major Symptoms: Violent temper tantrums .
Diagnosis: Pre-clinical hypogeusia
Possible Cause: Corn and most corn products, high-fibre foods, especially bran; meat fed on copper-supplemented feed; peanuts; potatoes; soya beans and soya bean products, including meat extenders.

Dr. Carl Pfeiffer, one of the first nutrition scientists to link minerals to brain function, noted that Fran couldn't see things clearly and without distortion, forgot what was told her, had trouble learning, was chronically irritable, and was extremely antagonistic and uncooperative much of the time. But what particularly marked her disorder, Dr. Pfeiffer wrote, was "unprovoked temper tantrums involving ranting and raving [and] cruel swear words".

Before Fran's parents brought her to Dr. Pfeiffer in 1975, they had placed their daughter in the hands of psychiatrists, psychological counsellors, and paeeiatricians with no results. But as soon as they told Dr. Pfeiffer the only time Fran was normal was after she had eaten fried oysters, he had the answers.

Oysters are rich in zinc, and they had temporarily wiped out the zinc deficiency that had triggered less intense symptoms of the zinc-deprivation disease, hypogeusia. Pointing out to her parents that Fran couldn't eat fried oysters three times a day for the rest of her life, he prescribed a zinc supplement in an amount appreciably higher than the RDA.

"The very next day they gave her the first dose of zinc", Dr. Pfeiffer wrote, "[and] she was positively improved. Within two weeks after she had started the zinc . . . the parents [were] enjoying the new Fran. [They were saying] 'she has a great sense of humour, is considerate and fun to be around.' She was always unusually alert and cooperative—and never had any tantrums".

But when, after three and a half months, her zinc supplements were discontinued, Fran "had a 'blow-up'—a real temper tantrum . . . including ranting alone in her room", Dr. Pfeiffer wrote. "In a week . . . her behaviour had deteriorated so much that [the parents] had to resume [zinc supplements].

"They gave her the first zinc capsule at 8.30 A.M.", Dr. Pfeiffer wrote. Then they watched and waited in a state of high anxiety to see if it would work again. By six that night their ordeal was over. Fran "was once again a changed person, and continued to be. 'There is no doubt whatsoever in our minds', the parents told Dr. Pfeiffer, 'that zinc had saved her'". Dr. Pfeiffer agreed. Because Fran had continued on a diet which probably contained foods that caused the zinc deficiency, ODA supplementation had to be continued.

Our Eating Plan for Brighter Kids (page 72), ODA-supplemented for zinc, lets them enjoy all the anti-zinc foods that we've already listed in Fran's case history summary.

CHAPTER 6

THE AVERAGE DIET

Are Today's Fresh Foods as Bad as Junk Foods for Your Kids' Brains?

The average diet for kids today is 80 per cent junk food and 20 per cent natural foods. Nutrition-minded parents, seeking a way to better the average, have cheered the appearance of rehabilitated junk foods—those with no or low sugar, salt, fat and additives; and those that are 'all natural'. They've also raised the percentage of *real* natural foods in their families' diets. But, sadly, most rehabilitated junk foods and most fresh foods are not as safe and sound as they seem.

Only a small number of rehabilitated junk foods meet the no-harm test, and most of our natural foods are in their own way as dangerously processed as junk foods. On the average diet, no matter how hard you try, there is no way you can feed your kids to brightness, or to better health.

The evidence for that statement—highlights follow—is so compelling that you'll want to change your children's diet at once. It's the evidence that motivated us when we created our Eating Plan for Brighter Kids.

Aren't There Any Good Junk Foods?

Read the labels, and you'll find them perverse prescriptions for bringing on almost all the mental disorders now associated with food: colouring, flavourings, preservatives, and other chemical additives that could afflict your kids with hyperactivity; sugar that could turn your kids in Jekyll and Hydes; caffeine (mainly in cola drinks and chocolate) that could lift your kids high then drop them to the bottom of the class; excess salt that, neurobiologists now claim, could over-excite your kids' brains; excess saturated fats that could slow them down.

Consider *no/low/less-sugar* foods. With some exceptions, they're laden with salt, additives, saturated fats, and substitute sweeteners that can be harmful, or more harmful, than sugar. No-sugar soft drinks go cloudy without sugar, and something has to be added to give the crystal-clear sales appeal. That something is stannous chloride, and it can harm your kids' brains and nervous systems.

Consider *no/low/less-salt (sodium) foods*. Most of these are glutted with sugar or sugar substitutes and a gross mix of additives and saturated fats as you can find in any unreformed junk food. Low-sodium canned soups and most dry soup mixes are flagrant examples.

When sodium from sources other than salt (say, from mono-*sodium* glutamate [MSG] is cut down in a food, more salt is usually added. So, there may not be a grain of MSG in some sausages anymore, but most are as salty as pickles. They're also stuffed with saturated fats and additives.

Consider *no/low/less-fat foods*. These are crammed with almost all the junk that gives junk food its bad name—including saturated fats. Some health-food yoghurt products—yoghurt raisins, for example—are homogenized with highly saturated palm and coconut oils. (Oils are fats that are liquid at room temperature.)

Consider *no/low/less-additives foods*. Some cut down on the number of additives, but one additive to a susceptible child could be as harmful as two dozen. Some truly include no additives during processing, but most of the foods have been treated chemically *before* they're processed—on the farm or in the orchards—and the additives are built-in. Your apple juice container may read PURE—NO ADDITIVES, but apples come to the juice extractors already treated with pesticides, fungicides, colouring agents, and growth-control chemicals.

At bottom, no contemporary processed food can truly be called natural because the very processing denaturalizes it—pillages it of the nutrients nature gave it. Canning destroys up to 80 per cent of some minerals and up to 100 per cent of some vitamins, according to Dr. Henry Schroeder, a pre-eminent authority on the nutrient content of foods. Freezing is almost as devastating.

Milling denudes gsain of many vitamins and minerals states Dr. Bernard Rimland, "there are well over twenty nutrients which lose 80 per cent or so of their value in the milling process, and [the lost values of] only four of those twenty or so are replaced". In a famous experiment conducted by the renowned pioneer medical nutrition scientist Dr. Roger J. Williams at the University of Texas, two-thirds of just-weaned rats on an 'enriched' white-bread diet died in three months and the remaining one-third were abnormal. "If this 'food' ", comments Dr. Michael Colgan, "cannot support the life of a rat, a very tough, adaptable creature, then it certainly cannot support the life of a human child".

The Best of the Rehabilitated Junk Foods

These products eliminate additives or limit them to one or just a few of the harmless ones (like BHT in shredded wheat), and contain no added sugar and little or no added salt. The canned foods on this list, although lacking the higher vitamin/mineral content of their natural counterparts, are sugar-free and salt-free or low in added salt, and are tasty additions to a well balanced and fully supplemented diet. We include the best of the rehabilitated junk foods in our Eating Plan for Brighter Kids.

Baking powder, without aluminium
    (a mineral that could be harmful to your
    child's body and brain)
Canned pineapple in unsweetened pineapple
    juice
Canned salmon, sardines, and tuna, no salt
    added, packed in water
Canned whole tomatoes, tomato juice, tomato
    paste,
    tomato purée, no salt added
Dijon mustard, no salt or sugar added
Familia (Swiss Birchermuesli), the no-salt,
    no-sugar version of this breakfast food
Grain coffees (caffeine-free substitutes)*
Jams and jellies, unsweetened
Low-fat cheeses, low in salt
Pasta, salt-free and without additives—not new,
    but new in popularity
Peanut butter, unhydrogenated, unsalted,
    preferably freshly made
Rice crackers, Oriental, unsalted
Shredded wheat, including all new varieties
Soy sauce, sodium-reduced
Vegetable seasonings, low in salt

*For flavouring (as used in my recipes, grain coffees don't taste like coffee, so kids can't get hooked on the taste) and for adult enjoyment instead of real coffee.

The New Tragedy for Your Kids: Processed Fresh Foods

The processing of fresh foods begins in the soil. Treated with chemical growth-stimulants for decades, "our topsoil is becoming deficient", warns one the nation's leading child care specialists, Dr. Lendon Smith, former clinical professor of Paediatrics at the University of Oregon Medical School. "Even if we eat well, it is not a guarantee that we will get the minimum amount of minerals our bodies must have to function properly".

The minerals lacking in some soils include iodine, iron, and zinc, whose deficiencies in kids' diets have been associated with pre-clinical and clinical mental/emotional problems and learning disabilities. Other minerals in short supply include calcium, copper, selenium, fluoride, and molybdenum. These, like the other three, are not only vital to a healthy body/brain for your kids, but also play important roles in the synthesis by plants of those vitamins, particularly of the B-complex, whose deficiencies can cripple the learning abilities of some children.

Grown nutrient-poor, some of our fruits and vegetables are further drained of nutrients by chemical control drugs that "promote uniform size, delay ripening so harvesting can take place at one time, intensify the colour . . . and extend shelf life by two to three months", the U.S. Federal Environmental Protection Agency (EPA) reported in 1985. Millions of pounds of chemical control drugs are used yearly by growers of apples, Brussels sprouts, canteloupes, cherries, grapes, peaches, peanuts, prune plums, and tomatoes.

Unripe produce is also an economic plus to agribusiness because these foods are harvested in the shortest time at the lowest cost, and they can endure on shelves longer before they rot. But unripe food has not had the time to manufacture its full quota of vitamins and other nutrients, and is not likely to do so after severance from the soil (bananas are the exception). The false ripe look of artificially coloured produce is a cruel deception to parents who have come to regard fruit and vegetables as 'good for their kids'.

Another form of plant-food processing, refrigeration during shipping and storage to extend shelf life, takes a heavy toll on temperature-sensitive vitamins. Dr. Michael Colgan provides these examples: lettuce, one day after it's picked, loses 50 per cent of its vitamin C, and in three more days of subnormal temperature loses 50 per cent of the remaining vitamins, for a total loss of 75 per cent. "Asparagus, broccoli, and green beans", he adds, "also lose . . . vitamin C in cold storage—50 per cent *before* they reach your green-grocer" (emphasis ours).

Processing exacts its own toll on our fresh animal food in many of the ways it does on our plant food. In two ways, though, the effects of processing can be worse. Synthetic hormones in feeds help manufacture the most edible meat at the lowest production cost, but the meat is supersaturated with fat, and abnormal in nutritive values. Antibiotics, processed into cattle, pigs, turkey, and chicken, can induce allergic reactions, sometimes cerebral, in some kids, and may be goitrogenic – that is reduce the absorption of iodine from other foods.

To the degradation of fresh food by the fresh food industry, add contamination from general industrial pollution. Mercury, cadmium, copper, aluminium, and lead in air, water, and soil infiltrate some of our fresh food at toxic levels, attacking children's bodies and brains directly, and by depriving them of vitamins and other essential minerals. It is no wonder that the metal poisoning of our foods is associated with some of the most common mental diseases of today's children.

CHAPTER 7

THE HIGH-CARBOHYDRATE DIET, THE WELL-BALANCED DIET

What's the Right Diet for Your Kids' Brains?

The leading alternatives to the average junk food diet are the high-carbohydrate diet and the well balanced diet. The high-carbohydrate diet is at the same time a low-protein, low-fat diet. The well-balanced diet, an invention of medical nutrition scientists at the U.S. Department of Agriculture (USDA) provides, as its name implies, an optimal balance—not too high, not too low—of carbohydrates, proteins, and fats.

Both of these well-respected diets may be harmful to your kids' brains. But one of them, the well-balanced diet, brought up to date and with the harmful factors removed, forms the base for the best possible diet not only for your children but for your whole family. It is the foundation diet for our Eating Plan for Brighter Kids.

Why the High-Carbohydrate Diet Can Harm Your Kids' Brains

Carbohydrates are one of the three classes of foods contributing energy (calories) to the human body/brain. They are found mainly in plant foods—vegetables, fruits, grains, pulses, and the products made from them. Indispensable to your kids' health and growth when consumed in the right amounts, they can lead to deficiency when they dominate the diet.

The RDA of carbohydrates for school kids is about 53 per cent of the diet in terms of total calories but some nutrition scientists consider 60 to 75 per cent healthful. When the diet goes beyond 75 per cent, it could be hazardous to your child. It is that kind of diet that we refer to as 'the high-carbohydrate diet'.

A high-carbohydrate diet can create iron deficiency, leading to dullness in kids' brains:

Iron deficiency dulls a child's brain because the body lacks the right amount of iron to manufacture sufficient haemoglobin, the substance in red blood cells that transports oxygen to the brain. The brain doesn't get enough oxygen, and this is what results:

Learning disabilities. Memory Loss. Diminished attention span. Irritability. Sluggishness. Fatigue. Lack of motivation. All are pre-clinical symptoms of anaemia. (Anaemia is a disease of varied symptoms characterized by sickly red blood cells and a low red blood cell count).

So devastating are the effects of brain oxygen shortage on a young child, even after it's corrected, that Dr. Ian Holzman, infant-care specialist at the Magee-Woman's Hospital, Pittsburgh, warns that early iron deficiency "could have significant [negative] implication in terms of learning and scholastic achievements" in later life.

No nutrition disorder is more widespread among young children than iron deficiency. We now know that anti-iron foods are one of its causes. This identification has come mainly as a result of the extensive and meticulous studies conducted by the medical nutrition scientists of the International National Anaemia Consultative Group (INACG). A list of anti-iron foods, compiled from INACG data, appears below.

Anti-iron foods are harmful only on a high-carbohydrate diet, since they can successfully attack iron in plant foods (non-haem iron) but not in animal foods (haem iron). On a vegetarian diet, the presence of anti-iron foods means an iron-deficiency diet.

INACG warns, particularly, against a diet high in soya beans and soya bean products, especially cereal-soya blends

---

Foods That Can Cause Iron-Deficiency Brain Dullness in Your Kids

These foods are harmless when animal foods are a regular part of your kids' diet, since anti-iron foods attack only iron present in plants (non-haem iron). Anti-iron foods on a pure vegetarian diet, which is low in iron to begin with, can be dangerous to your kids physically as well as mentally.

Anti-Iron Foods	Natural Anti-Iron Chemicals in the Foods
Bran	
Cereals	Phytates
Cheese	Phytates
Corn	Phosphates
Black-eyed peas	Phytates
Eggs	Polyphenols
Millet	Phosphates
Broad beans	Polyphenols
Pulses	Polyphenols
Milk, cow's*	Polyphenols
Rice	Phosphates
Spinach	Phytates
Soya beans	Polyphenols
Tea†	Phytates and saponins
	Polyphenols
Wine, red†	Polyphenols

* This emphasizes the need of iron supplements for infants on formula milks, and for children who drink cow's milk.
† If you need another reason for eliminating these beverages from your kids' diet, here it is.

---

such as soya milk—a potent combination of anti-iron foods. The special danger, as INACG sees it, is that since soya beans are higher in protein than other vegetables, they are widely used as inexpensive substitutes for animal protein to create a pure vegetarian diet with built-in iron destructive capacity.

All anti-iron foods are harmless on a diet that supplies adequate amounts of meat, poultry, or fish. Meat, which is particularly high in haem iron, also increases the body's ability to use non-haem iron in the potatoes and other vegetables with which the meat is served. That's one reason meat—especially red meat, the highest in iron of all animal foods—is included in our Eating Plan for Brighter Kids.

Pre-clinical symptoms of anaemia itself, can also be induced on high-carbohydrate diets due to the virtual absence of vitamin B_{12} (cobalamin) and the extremely low levels of two other vitamins of the B-complex—vitamin B_6 (pyridoxine) and folic acid. All three vitamins are indispensable for the manufacture of haemoglobin.

These vitamins are supplied in the animal foods of our Eating Plan for Brighter Kids, and brought up to ODA (Optimal Dietary Allowance) levels with the *right* amounts of supplements. (Taken in excess, iron may stimulate bacterial growth). Our Plan is also rich in vitamin C (ascorbic acid), vital to the utilization of iron in the body/brain.

A high-carbohydrate diet can create deficiencies in six minerals, leading to kids' brain dullness:

A high-carbohydrate diet need not be high in fibre, but today it usually is. Fibre is what we used to call 'roughage'. Fixed in the public's mind by media medical experts as 'healthful', high-roughage diets can be rough on your kids.

Fibre is an indigestible carbohydrate (think of wood) that contributes no energy (calories) and no nutrients. It plays a necessary role in our digestive processes, helping to prevent constipation, and by biochemical pathways still unknown, it is purported to prevent a spectrum of diseases as different as tooth decay and diabetes.

The normal diet for older school kids contains a estimated 6 to 10 grams (around a quarter of an ounce) of 'dietary fibre' a day. (Dietary fibre describes all non-nutrient carbohydrates, as opposed to 'crude fibre', which is applied to only two kinds). High fibre advocates recommended as much as 50 grams of dietary fibre daily—and that could be much too much for your kids.

At that level, fibre blocks the absorption of brain-vital

minerals calcium, copper, iron, magnesium, phosphorus, and zinc. The result: your kids can be afflicted by one, or any grouping, of the following pre-clinical symptoms: irritability; nervousness; insomnia; mood swings; anxiety; depression; memory loss; diminished attention span; impaired sense perceptions; sluggishness; fatigue; lack of motivation; learning disability.

It seems quite right then for the Food and Nutrition Board, National Academy of Sciences—National Research Council, to recommend that "marked increases in dietary fibre should be avoided". Alice White, the noted children's nutritionist, adds another reason for curbing fibre consumption: "high-fibre foods tend to be low in calories, and since your children have small stomachs, emphasis on these foods might not provide your child with adequate calories"—and without adequate calories, the supply of all nutrients is inadequate.

"Parents should add fibre to meals in moderation," cautions Boston Children's Hospital, the largest paediatric medical centre in the U.S. Our Eating Plan for Brighter Kids limits the amount of high-fibre foods to moderate, healthful levels.

High Fibre Foods That May Harm Your Kids' Brain

High fibre foods (below) in moderation are healthy, but prolonged consumption of above-optimal quantities can hurt your child mentally and physically. Excess fibre impairs the absorption of brain-vital minerals, and, attacked by intestinal bacteria, it can produce noxious gases in the digestive tract with pain, vomiting, and nausea.

Beans (especially lima); green beans
Berries (especially raspberries)
Bran cereals; whole-wheat cereals
Broccoli; Brussels sprouts
Dried fruit (especially figs and raisins)
Fresh fruits (especially plums, pears, and apples
   with the skin)
Pulses (especially peas); corn
Nuts (especially almonds); coconut
Potatoes (especially baked with the skin)
Salad greens

PART III

The Nutrition/Brightness Revolution in Brain Research

CHAPTER 8

THE BIRTH OF YOUR CHILD'S BRAIN

Feeding Yourself Right and Your Kids Bright During Pregnancy

In the last ten years or so, a new breed of scientists, the neurobiologists, have discovered more about how your child's brain grows in your womb than humankind had learned in all its previous long years on earth.

In practical terms, this revolutionary new knowledge provides you for the first time with a guide to the foods of pregnancy that help you give birth not only to a healthy child but to a bright child. It keys you to:

- the best foods for growing your child's brain cells (billions of them) and the amazing communications network that connects them
- the best foods for building a special group of brain cells that increase your unborn child's brain power (the glial-cell complex; Albert Einstein, for instance, had a larger than average glial-cell complex)
- the best foods for providing your unborn child's brain

cells with the energy to grow on (they have to supply just the *one* nutrient your baby's brain will accept)

- the best food supplements, because without them all the other 'bests' would be second bests
- and the worst foods that, if relied on mainly during pregnancy, could harm your baby's brain.

Remember: during pregnancy, what *you* eat is what your unborn child's brain grows on. When you eat bright, you eat right for yourself—including a surprising plus: you may not have to gain all the weight most doctors say is unavoidable (see pages 62 and 63).

The Best Foods for Growing Your Unborn Child's Brain Cells and the Brain's Communication Network

The brain is protein territory. The basic brain cell (the neutron) is mainly protein. The part of the brain cell that carries messages like a telephone wire (the axon) is a protein. So are the parts that send messages to other cells (the axon terminals) and receive messages from other cells (the dendrites). The remarkable biochemicals that activate brain messages (the neurotransmitters) are proteins, The substance in the brain that manages the growth of this total communications network, the Nerve Growth Factor, NGF, is a protein.

Should you go on a high-protein diet during pregnancy?

You should not. For decades doctors prescribed high-protein pregnancy diets (they have only discontinued the practice in the last several years), and none of the kids were any brighter for it. (The doctors weren't trying for brighter kids; they were trying to prevent a common pregnancy disorder, toxaemia. They didn't).

Actually, the growing brain can handle just so much protein, and blocks the rest. What your kid's brain needs is not massive doses of protein, but the right amounts of the right proteins. The right amounts are easily obtained from animal food—meat, fish, poultry, and plain yoghurt—from about a quarter pound a day for a 100-pound woman to about a half a pound for a 165-pound woman (weights are pre-pregnancy). These animal foods also supply the right proteins.

They're called 'complete proteins' because they contain in the right proportions the complete complement of the amino acids your kid's growing body and brain needs from foods.

These are the 'essential amino acids', and you can find out just how important they are to your kid's brain from the chart on page 53.

Are vegetable proteins as good for your unborn child as animal proteins?

Most plants do not contain all the amino acids. Some plant foods contain some of them; some contain others. In the plant foods that do contain all the amino acids, the proportions are wrong for human needs. The only way to obtain proteins for your unborn child from plant foods is to combine specific selections from the vegetable kingdom that together provide all the essential amino acids in the right proportions.

Here is a sampling of such combinations, They're called *complementary proteins*:

Rice and sesame seeds

Rice and tofu

Rice and beans

Rice and lentils

Beans and peas

Beans and wholemeal
bread

Beans and cracked wheat

Beans and cornmeal

Beans and corn bread

Beans and tortillas

Chickpeas and tahini
(sesame-seed paste)

Soya beans (roasted),
sunflower seeds, and
peanuts

Lentils and barley

Split peas and corn bread

Whether it's prudent on a pregnancy diet to replace complete animal proteins with complementary vegetable proteins is a matter of controversy. In favour are the nutritionists who point out that in some animal protein-impoverished countries, diets of complimentary proteins—such as rice and beans, or corn-based tortillas and beans—provide the amino acids essential to unborn children. Patricia Houseman, formerly staff nutritionist at the Centre for Science in the Public Interest, Washington, D.C., writes that "the record shows that vegetable protein *can* meet the protein needs of . . . pregnant and nursing women" (emphasis ours).

But the opponents of a vegetarian diet point out that a high-carbohydrate diet may prevent amino acids from reaching the unborn child's brain. This diet is also likely to be low in the vitamin folic acid and the minerals calcium, iron, and zinc, all necessary for the construction of brain proteins from amino acids.

Essential Amino Acids: The Brain Brighteners

For any of the amino acids to be effective, all must be present in the body/brain in optimal amounts. Those amounts of essential amino acids are supplied by the animal and vegetable foods of our Eating Plan for Brighter Kids. Because of the chance of overdosage from amino acid supplements with consequent harm to kids' brains, these supplements should not be given to kids, and should not be taken by you during pregnancy and breastfeeding. The essential amino acids listed here are essential for children; not all are essential for adults.

Arginine releases the growth hormone (GH) which is crucial to brain and body growth.

Cystine/Cysteine helps protect against mental disorders.

Glutamine stimulates mental activity, diminishes confusion, improves memory and learning ability.

Glycine produces a calming effect in stress situations.

Histidine promotes brain growth.

Isoleucine helps prevent mental retardation.

Leucine improves mental activity and fights mental disorders.

Lysine helps the brain utilize calcium, a mineral vital to neuronal functioning.

Methionine combats stress and fatigue, and helps ward off mental disorders.

Phenylalanine strengthens neurotransmitter signals. With tyrosine, it promotes alertness, ambition, and positive feelings—including feelings of joy.

Taurine improves memory.

Threonine contributes to normal brain functioning.

Tryptophan stabilizes emotions, reverses depression, suppresses irrational anger, and normalizes sleep patterns.

Tyrosine boosts intelligence, helps control anxiety and depression, provides a lift from fatigue. (See *Phenylalanine*).

Valine promotes mental vigour, dissipates negative emotions.

In addition, a pure vegetarian diet contains virtually no vitamin B_{12}, leading to brain-damaging pre-clinical and clinical anaemia. And recently discovered is the association of mental disorders with severe vitamin-A deficiency in the diets of unborn children in animal protein-impoverished countries. Boston Children's Hospital, basing its conclusion on physical health hazards alone, asserts that "vegan diets which omit all sources of animal protein . . . are not suitable and, in fact, are dangerous for growing children".

Three compromise diets, devoid of animal flesh but containing some animal food, hold out the promise of complete protein without the drawbacks of a pure vegetarian diet. They are: the lacto-ovo-vegetarian diet. 'Lacto' means milk and cheese; 'ovo' means eggs, and vegetarian means vegetables, fruits, grains and pulses plus nuts. the *lacto-vegetarian diet* excludes eggs, and features milk and cheese with any of the following: potatoes, beans, rice, peanuts, or wheat. The *ovo-vegetarian diet* substitutes eggs for milk and cheese. All these diets include products made from the basic ingredients.

These diets are basically sound, but since the match of plant foods with animal foods must be made with extreme care to provide complete proteins, they are not recommended during pregnancy unless under doctor/nutritionist supervision.

Should you get the essential amino acids your unborn child needs from amino acid supplements?

No. Your unborn child's brain can shut out excess amino acids from protein *foods*, but it cannot shut out excess amino acids from *supplements*. Excess quantities of amino acids may induce overexcitement in the growing brain, leading at birth to a child prone to mental disorders as serious as hyperactivity, and intense anxiety leading to panic.

That's one reason some nutrition scientists recommend banning from your kitchen the sweetener aspartame, even though it's FDA approved. It's actually an amino acid supplement composed of two amino acids, phenylalanine and aspartic acid. Boston Children's Hospital reports that "consumer advocacy groups . . . contend that the body cannot metabolize . . . high concentrations of amino acids efficiently, and that health problems, even brain damage . . . may result if growing children use too much aspartame".

Amino acids are best derived from the protein in your diet. But be careful:

- Don't binge on a high-carbohydrate meal. The carbohydrates stimulate the flow of insulin, and that expels most of the amino acids from your bloodstream before they can reach your unborn child's brain.
- Stay away from the sprouts of haricot, and kidney beans. They interfere with the body's metabolic processes that extract the amino acids from protein food. Most sprouts are healthful, but these can deprive your unborn child's brain of essential amino acids.

How can you benefit during pregnancy from the right amounts of the right proteins?

These help you to a successful pregnancy in the following ways: by providing normal growth of your breasts, blood volume, and uterus; building stronger enzyme, hormone, haemoglobin, and immune systems; and by producing optimal quantities of amniotic fluid, the colourless liquid that protects your baby during gestation.

Guidelines to Protein Sources for Your Pregnancy Diet

These are the guidelines we followed in creating our Eating Programme for Brighter Kids.

The Best Protein Foods: animal foods—meats, fish, poultry, eggs, cheese, milk, and plain yoghurt; and complementary vegetable foods (see list on page 52). These foods supply the essential amino acids for your unborn child's growing brain.

The Worst Protein Foods: vegetable foods when they're not complemented—vegetables, fruits, grains, and pulses. These foods lack some of the essential amino acids on which your child's brain will grow. However, foods from the vegetable kingdom are indispensable on a well-balanced pregnancy diet to provide energy for the growth of your child's brain.

The Best Foods for Increasing Your Unborn Child's Brain Power

Associated with I.Q., the glial-cell complex of the brain

strengthens your unborn child's brain power in several ways. The complex is a storehouse of nutrients—of amino acids, vitamins, and minerals for building neurons and the brain's communications network; and of glucose to power brain growth and activity. It helps form a superthick 'blood-brain' barrier, that keeps out many substances in the blood that could dim the developing brain. It provides the insulation for the brain's wiring system that strengthens the electrical impulses that 'fire' the brain's activity.

When the glial-cell complex is not constructed properly, your child could be born with an impaired brain. But constructed properly your child's brain could reach its maximum brightness. The glial-cell complex is constructed mostly of fats and cholesterol.

Should you go on a high-fat, high-cholesterol diet during pregnancy?

Yes, according to Dr. Ralph Minear, a leading authority on eating programmes for feeding kid's brains. With the growth needs of the glial-cell complex in mind, he sets the fat-consumption figure during pregnancy at 50 per cent of the diet in terms of total calories. He also holds that "cholesterol [is] obviously . . . absolutely essential . . . to the childs . . . proper brain development [and] mental well-being". Consumption of cholesterol after conception, he asserts, should not be curbed.

The position of Dr. Minear, who is a paediatrician at Harvard Medical School, is sharply at variance with that of most doctors who have established the low-fat, low cholesterol diet as a principle of good health. The diet, which is purported to fight atherosclerosis (which can lead to heart attack) and other degenerative disease including diabetes and cancer, contains sparse amounts of cholesterol and 20 per cent less fat than permitted by Dr. Minear.

How, then, can the high-fat/cholesterol recommendation of Dr. Minear be reconciled with the high-fat/cholesterol condemnation of virtually the rest of the medical profession? Dr. Minear answers, "There is a strong line of [medical] opinion that says giving a child significant amounts of cholesterol will help [the child's] body process it better later—and will . . . protect [the child] in . . . adult years against atherosclerosis". Other nutrition scientists believe that a fully vitamin/mineral-supplemented diet during pregnancy protect the mother and child from faulty fat/cholesterol metabolism that may lead to atherosclerosis.

"As for myself", Dr. Minear, who recommends full supplementation, states, "I'm convinced that the needs of [the child's] growing brain for fats and cholesterol . . . far outweighs any . . . fears about hardening of the arteries [atherosclerosis]". A low-fat/cholesterol diet may be beneficial to adults and older children, Dr. Minear concludes, but a high-fat/cholesterol diet is beneficial to unborn and younger children.

What are the best fats for your unborn child's growing brain?
There are three kinds of fats. *Saturated fats*, which are found in meat and poultry, are implicated in the onset of atherosclerosis. *Polyunsaturated fats*, which are vegetable fats (except palm and coconut oils, which are saturated fats) have been recommended as a safe replacement for saturated fats; but recent evidence indicates that under certain circumstances they can change in the body and brain to destructive substances. The trend is now to opt for *monounsaturated fats*—some vegetable fats—such as olive oil and peanut oil—that seem to have no harmful effects.

However, the fats your child's growing brain needs must contain the essential fatty acids (EFAs)—linoleic, linolenic, and arachidonic— and all these fats are polyunsaturated. Nutrition scientists point out that they cannot be transformed to harmful substances in the body and brain when the diet is fully supplemented. The best sources of polyunsaturated fats are virgin vegetable oils (first-pressed) and fish.

Cholesterol is, contrary to popular belief, not a fat, but a waxy alcohol. It's found in animal fats. There's no cholesterol in the vegetable kingdom. That's another reason a pure vegetarian diet during pregnancy is dangerous to your child's brain.

How can you benefit during pregnancy from the right amount of the right fats?
Fats are necessary for the structural changes in your body to prepare for the birth and nursing of your child, particularly the enlargement of the uterus and breasts. Cutting down on fats during pregnancy, from the physiological viewpoint alone, can be harmful to both you and your child. Don't regard this as a licence to gorge on fatty foods. Follow the moderate guidelines of our Eating Plan for Brighter Kids.

The Best Foods for Providing Your Unborn Child's Brain with the Energy to Grow On

Without glucose, the brain is powerless, literally without power. But when glucose is bonded with another substance in the brain, ATP, energy is generated that builds the brain and makes it run. Close down the flow of glucose, and brain activity dims and eventually dies. Glucose is a member of a class of foods called saccharides that includes sugars and starches. Sucrose, also a saccharide, breaks down in the body to fructose and glucose.

Is sucrose a good source of glucose, the brain's energy food?
    Not commercial sucrose—the pure, white crystalline sugar that has been stripped of every vitamin and mineral needed for its metabolism by the body. *That* sucrose is abnormally

metabolized, producing chemicals that could be harmful to your unborn child's (and your) body/brain.

But in nature, sucrose—in unprocessed fresh fruits, berries, and vegetables— is always packaged with the vitamins and minerals needed to be utilized normally by the body. The highest sucrose-content food of all, sugar cane, is brimful of vitamins and minerals necessary for metabolism, and it has been a tasty, nutritious staple of tropical peoples for millennia. (Perhaps it's time to revive it in our supermarkets as the 'new' health-food sweet).

Can you get your supply of glucose during pregnancy from glucose tablets?

No. Because the pure, white crystalline glucose in these tablets is empty calories, stripped of all the vitamins and minerals essential to its metabolism. Glucose tablets can be as harmful to your unborn child's brain as pure sucrose.

All naturally occurring saccharides are converted in the body to glucose, so look for your best sources of glucose in foods which supply the most glucose from the saccharides. You'll find a list of those foods on this page. It's based on the studies of Dr. Arne Dahlqvist, professor and chairman of nutrition, the University of Lund, Sweden.

The Best Sources of Glucose—the Nutrient That Powers Your Unborn Child's Brain Growth and Function

Although most of the foods on this list do not contain glucose as such, they metabolize to glucose in the body. The 'glucose value' represents the amount of glucose supplied by a food compared to that supplied by pure glucose, which has a glucose value of 100. Do not settle on just one of these foods for its high glucose value, but eat a variety of them to obtain a maximum mix of other nutrients.

Food	Type of Saccharide	Glucose Value
Fruits	Glucose, fructose,	
Berries	sucrose	80 to 95
Grains	Glucose, fructose,	
Vegetables	sucrose	80 to 95

Potatoes	Starch	65 to 90
Mushrooms	Starch, sucrose	60 to 90
Milk	Starch	80
Oysters	Starch	40 to 50
Liver	Lactose	30 to 50
	Glycogen	20 to 25
	Glycogen	10

How can you benefit during pregnancy from high glucose-value foods?

These power-packed foods provide the energy for the structural and hormonal changes necessary for a successful pregnancy. They also help prevent one of the common complaints of pregnant women—'that worn-out feeling'.

Guidelines to Glucose Sources for Your Pregnancy Diet

These are the guidelines we followed in creating our Eating Programme for Brighter Kids.

The Best Glucose Foods: see the table above.

The Worst Glucose Foods: pure white, crystalline sucrose, glucose, and other sugars, and their products. All animal foods except oysters, milk, animal livers. But animal foods are otherwise essential and are part of our balanced pregnancy menus.

The Best Vitamin Supplements for Getting the Most from the Best Foods During Pregnancy

The nutrients with which you feed your unborn child bright and yourself right during pregnancy—complete proteins, essential amino and fatty acids, cholesterol and high-glucose foods—cannot be utilized fully without vitamins and minerals present in your body at full strength. Vitamins and minerals are 'co-factors' that enter into the biochemical processes building your unborn child's body/brain, and prepare your body for childbirth.

That deficiencies in vitamins and minerals during pregnancy can adversely affect your child's mental health has been well established. Dr. Michael Colgan, as a result of a survey conducted in 1983, reported that "the diets of teenage girls are seriously deficient in calcium, iron, magnesium, and vitamin B_6. . . . For the pregnant among these girls, their babies risk . . . mental retardation".

On the other hand, complete supplementation during pregnancy could help you give birth to a potentially bright child. Dr. Josep Brožek of the Psychology Department, Lehigh University, Pennsylvania, reviewing the scientific literature over the last fifteen years on the nutrition/brightness link, concludes that pre-natal supplementation improves a child's mental performance later in life, particularly in the areas of memory, language, and perception.

When should you start to take vitamin/mineral supplements, and in what amounts?

Progressive nutrition scientists hold that supplementation should begin prior to conception to compensate for ODA-vitamin/mineral deficiencies suffered by most women on typical diets. Bringing vitamin/minerals in the body up to ODA levels, these scientists agree, helps you enter pregnancy in optimal health to produce a bright and healthy child.

During pregnancy, however, some doctors recommend RDA supplements lest higher amounts have an adverse effect on the unborn child's growing brain. Dr. Bernard Rimland dissents. "There is no evidence for this", he writes, "except that truly *massive* amounts of vitamin A could produce defects in a small number of sensitive individuals" (emphasis his).

He reports one study in which pregnant women were provided with 10,000 milligrams of vitamin C a day instead of the pregnancy RDA of 60 milligrams. "The children were unusually bright and healthy. And none were retarded". The same study, and others, also revealed an advantage to the pregnant women from high vitamin-C dosage: "the duration of labour was cut by half".

Dr. Rimland also holds that the much-publicized claim that "megadoses of vitamin B_6 taken by pregnant women will lead to vitamin-B_6 dependency in the offspring is not proven and probably incorrect". For pregnant women, he concludes, "I would certainly opt for Optimal Dietary Allowance [ODA] levels".

How can you benefit from taking all the right vitamins and minerals in the right amounts during pregnancy?

Aside from maintenance of your wellness, and the natural high that comes from good nutrition, you can benefit from it in a surprisingly pleasant way. It can help you keep your weight down. Here are the facts:

During pregnancy a woman's vitamin and mineral needs increase (even pregnancy RDAs are higher then non-pregnancy RDAs). To meet these needs, pregnant women eat more; and the increased calorie consumption accounts for most of the weight gain.

On the average pregnancy diet of the early 1950s, built mainly on non-processed foods naturally rich in vitamins and minerals, the increase in calories necessary to supply the vitamin/mineral needs of pregnancy resulted in weight gains of only 10 to 15 pounds. But as the food processing industry progressively cut the vitamin/mineral content of food, it became necessary for women to eat more *and more* to obtain their pregnancy vitamin/mineral ODAs. Weight gains during pregnancy mounted. By the early 1960s, the medically approved weight gain had soared to 20 pounds; by the early 1970s to 24 to 27 pounds; and currently it's at an all-time high of 30 pounds.

While most non-pregnant women consume 1,200 to 1,600 calories a day, many doctors recommend 2,600 to 2,800 calories for pregnant women—which can result in prodigious weight gain (one slim woman added 68 pounds). Even the now 'normal' weight gain of 30 pounds is a burden to many women, who find the excess poundage put on easily during pregnancy is hard to take off afterwards.

A diet that leads to prolonged obesity is a health hazard. It should be avoided at any time. Studies by Dr. John Dobbing of the Manchester Medical School reveal that this may be avoided in pregnancy with 'increased dietary efficiency'—getting the most nutritive value out of just-right amounts of foods. This may be accomplished by a sound balanced diet, fully supplemented. In this way, a woman could consume her pregnancy ODAs, and be "relieved of the need to eat more during pregnancy" to obtain them. Whether 'increased dietary efficiency' can restore average pregnancy weight gains to the 10-to-15 pound level of the 1950s is still to be determined. But the new concept holds out hope for today's weight-conscious mothers-to-be.

A word of caution: before you go on a fully supplemented

diet during pregnancy—and especially if you desire to control your weight—it is mandatory to consult a paediatrician who is trained and experienced in nutrition.

CHAPTER 9

THE SECOND BIRTH OF YOUR CHILD'S BRAIN

The Bright Foods of Infancy and Early Childhood

Most children are born with about 10 billion basic brain cells (neurons). But after birth not a single neuron will ever be born again. If for any reason, nutritional or otherwise, your child is born with less than the full quota of neurons, there's no cause to despair. Nature has built a fail-safe mechanism. In essence, your child's brain is born for a second time—after birth.

According to Dr. Changeux, professor of Neurobiology at the College de France, Paris, and a leader in the recent triumphs of brain research concerning children, the second birth involves the natural construction of a 'new' brain using the billions of neurons with which your child was born.

This involves an intricate growth process, according to Dr. Changeux, in which three basic elements of the brain proliferate to form 'pathways in the brain'—communication circuits with which your child talks, feels, thinks, acts. These 'pathways'—in an almost infinite variety—transform the virtually unorganized brain at birth into the amazing machine with which your child will perceive the world and react to it.

The three basic elements that multiply enormously after birth are the glial-cell complex, the neurotransmitters, and the dendrites. For glial-cell expansion your child's brain needs fats and cholesterol; for neurotransmitters and dendrites, proteins; for the energy of growth, glucose. And for the co-factors that activate all these nutrients, your child needs the full quota of vitamins and minerals. The nutritional demands of your child's brain after birth—and for three to five years thereafter as the new brain grows faster than it ever will again—are fundamentally the same as they were during pregnancy, only intensified.

How is your infant and your young child to be fed during this period? Nature has developed the perfect food—mother's milk. But if you plan to discontinue breastfeeding after at most six months, as many mothers do, don't worry—our Eating Plan for Brighter Kids provides a basic nutritional equivalent of mother's milk for the full span of the second birth of your child's brain.

Breastfeeding: The Best Way to Feed Your Infant to Brightness

The current position of the medical profession, as reflected by Dr. William C. McClean, Jr., clinical associate professor of Paediatrics at Ohio State University, is "Human milk is a *complete* food able to meet the nutritional requirements of the newborn and older infant. . . .*There is no doubt that breastfeeding is preferred for the infant*" (emphasis ours).

Mother's milk has been perfectly bioengineered by nature to satisfy all the nutritional needs of the second birth of your child's brain. It contains all the essential amino acids in the right proportions. (The wrong proportions can stunt brain growth, distort neurotransmitter balance, and lead to brain disorders). The quality of a protein is measured by how closely the proportions of its amino acids resemble proportions of amino acids in the human body. This comparison is called the biological value, and is rated on the basis of 0 to 100. Mother's milk has a biological value of 100 (Only egg white at 94 comes close).

Mother's milk contributes a rich supply of fats to support the rapid growth of the glial-cell complex, which nurtures and protects the explosively expanding pathways in the brain. The fats are mainly unsaturated, the kind not associated with heart attack. But these fats are vulnerable to attacks of 'oxidants', chemical fragments in the body/brain that can degenerate polyunsaturated fats into brain poisons. Mother's milk destroys these oxidants with an anti-oxidant nutrient team that includes vitamins A, E, C, B_1 and B_5; the minerals selenium, copper, and manganese; and the amino acids cystine and methionine.

Disturbing to the vast majority of doctors who now associate cholesterol with atherosclerosis and other degenerative diseases is the rich supply of cholesterol in mother's milk—a supply necessary to nurture the glial-cell complex. But cholesterol has been in mother's milk since the human race began without inducing those diseases. It's possible that mother's milk in well-nourished mothers contains a protective battery of vitamins and minerals that prevents faulty metabolism leading to the arterial deposits of cholesterol that are one of the causes of atherosclerosis.

Boston Children's Hospital reports that while cholesterol's "value to infants remains unclear . . . some experts have suggested it is necessary for the proper development of the nervous system". For that reason, and for others relating to overall health, the hospital strongly recommends that "*cholesterol should not be restricted in the diets of infants, and only moderately in young children's diets*" (emphasis theirs).

Lactose, the sugar in mother's milk, is readily converted in an infant's body to glucose, the brain's energy source. It has another quality that sets it apart from any sugar that's substituted for it in a formula. Absorbed slowly, it remains in the baby's intestine long enough to nurture those bacteria living there that benefit the infant in these ways: they fight off harmful bacteria; help in the absorption of minerals (including brain-vital calcium and magnesium); and manufacture B-complex vitamins, the group of vitamins most important in building the structures of the growing brain.

As they come to a child in mother's milk, the amino acids, the fats, cholesterol, and lactose, are packaged with substances (enzymes) for easy digestion. In a well-nourished mother, the milk is also vitamin/mineral rich, enabling the digested food to follow perfect metabolic pathways to sites where it's needed in the growing body/brain. (Unfortunately, many women are not well nourished, and babies fed on their milk, which is poor at least in vitamins C and folic acid and the mineral iron, must be supplemented).

Your infant also gains from breastfeeding in three other extraordinary ways: immunoglobulins, proteins that form the first line of defense against many viruses and bacteria, are present in the 'colostrum', the first fluid secreted by the breasts after birth. Immunoglobulins protect the infant from a wide range of dangerous diseases including flu, pneumonia, whooping cough, diphtheria, staphylococcal infections, polio, tetanus, salmonella, and gastroenteritis. In one study of 107 babies hospitalized for gastrointestinal disorders, 106 had not been breastfed. Not only is mother's milk not allergenic, it contains a substance that blocks the action of allergens, including brain allergens.

To blaze new pathways in the brain during the second birth of the baby's brain, stimulation is mandatory—and breastfeeding is the child's earliest stimulation, perhaps nature's way of starting and speeding the new brain growth. "Breast is best for a child's intellectual development", states Dr. Ralph Minear, "extremely important to the child's behaviour and emotional developments".

Dr. Miriam Stoppard, the renowned British expert on child care, adds experimental evidence. One group of laboratory monkeys, breastfed, grew normally. The other group, bottle-fed, grew up "moody, aggressive, quarrelsome, pugnacious, and generally troublesome". Comments Dr. Stoppard: "Similar problems arise with human babies".

What should a woman eat during breastfeeding?

Your infant's nutritional demands are fundamentally the same as during pregnancy, and they are satisfied in the same way—with the high-fat/cholesterol diet recommended by Dr. Minear, fully ODA-vitamin/mineral supplemented. This is the basis for the breastfeeding programme in our Eating Plan for Brighter Kids.

Can mothers benefit from breastfeeding?

In many ways:

- It's great for your figure. Breastfeeding releases hormones that quickly dissipate pregnancy fat, and return to normal the size and contours of uterus, pelvis, and waistline.
- It could be a natural contraceptive. The hormone that produces breast milk, prolactin, also suppresses ovulation. (But your doctor is likely to tell you not to rely on this fact).
- Breastfeeding may act as a cancer-preventive. In many countries in which breastfeeding is the norm, there is less breast cancer than in the United States.

- It can save you time and money. You don't have to prepare breast milk, buy the equipment to make it, or make it.
- It's dependable. "Infants are remarkably efficient at regulating their own diets", Boston Children's Hospital assures you. "When the baby is hungry, he or she makes this very clear". Wonderfully, *when* the baby makes this very clear, the breasts of a healthy mother naturally will have produced the right amount of milk to meet the demand. That's one reason many doctors recommend demand feeding to nursing mothers.

There is one benefit, though, that outshines all others. It's 'bonding', a transcendent emotional experience that is uniquely a woman's. When an infant suckles, when it feels the nourishment—life itself— flowing from you, and associates it with your closeness, your warmth, the perfume of your body, your touch, the light in your eyes, the embracing and the cuddling, a bond is forged that can enrich your life, and the life of your child, all your lives. It's the bond of love.

It's no wonder, then, that with all the natural benefits of breastfeeding, it has been the custom from time immemorial for mothers to keep their babies at their breast until the babies, no longer needing mother's milk, reject it. That time, throughout history, has been at about three years— corresponding to the major growth period of the child's brain after its second birth.

But in many countries, an arbitrary deadline for terminating breastfeeding is set at six months. Many women terminate even sooner. Of every 100 women who start breastfeeding in hospital, only 75 continue to breastfeed after two months; and only 46 after five months. At six months, the number plummets to virtually zero. (And for every 100 mothers who breasfeed at all, there's another 100 who never do).

But if mother's milk is the perfect food during the three years of the brain's second birth, how can kids be fed bright when they're deprived of it entirely or after six months at the most?

Feeding Your Kids to Brightness After Breastfeeding: The Mother's Milk Principle

The brilliantly simple solution came in 1983 from Dr. Ralph Minear of Harvard Medical School. He calls it the "Mother's

Milk Principle", and in essence it's this: you can feed your kids bright without mother's milk when you replace it with a diet whose basic nutritional composition closely resembles mother's milk.

Rejecting baby formula as a mother's milk substitute—"No formula can compare with mother's milk, either for a baby's general dietary needs or for the specific requirements of a child's growing brain"— and recognizing the futility of attempting to replace mother's milk with any other food— "It's impossible to find any single food that is the nutritional equivalent of breastfeeding for children up to 3 years of age"—Dr. Minear advocates:

"For at least the first 3 years of life—and in modified form up to the age of 5—the proportions of carbohydrates, fats, and proteins in the diet of a young child should come as close as possible to those of breast milk. This means that fat in the child's daily calorie consumption should range up to 50 per cent; complex carbohydrates should be 35 to 45 per cent; and proteins . . . should be 8 to 15 per cent". He observes, "In general, these values reflect what modern medical studies show to be the best brain food diet—and the best programme for overall nutrition as well".

He defends the high-fat content of his diet—15 to 20 per cent higher than in most doctor-recommended adult diets — saying, "Studies of the composition of human milk show it contains about 55 per cent fats", and adding, "Now it's true that some physicians have expressed concern that atherosclerosis . . . from too high a fat content in the blood may begin at a . . . young age. But there have been no studies that show there is any danger of feeding very young children fats in accordance with the Mother's Milk Principle. The fact is, a child needs more fats . . . at least up to the age of 3 and probably up to the age of 5 — largely because of the tremendous brain development that takes place during this time of life".

Whole milk, not skimmed milk, supplies these fats. For general health reasons, "young children need the fatty acids in whole milk", advises Boston Children's Hospital. "Skimmed milk it *not* better for children younger the two years old" (emphasis ours). At the age of 2, dendrites, essential for setting up connections between brain cells, reach their maximum number.

"Don't feed your pre-school child an adult diet that is low in fats", Dr. Minear advises parents. "Rather, if you want to

maximize your chances of increasing your child's brain power
. . . *keep the distribution of fats up around 50 per cent"* (emphasis his).

How do your feed your infant on the Mother's Milk Principle after *breastfeeding?*

This is how, based primarily on Dr. Minear's eating plan for infants, you can apply the Mother's Milk Principle to your baby's diet from 4 months to 1 year.

Months 4 and 5. During this time, you may introduce solid baby foods, although many doctors recommend 6 months as the starting date. But, cautions Boston Children's Hospital, do not begin before month 4. "Babies younger . . . are not developmentally ready for solid foods, and the agonies of such early feedings are wasted efforts because little food actually ends up in the baby".

Start with 1 to 2 teaspoons daily of an iron-fortified dry cereal mixed with breast milk (preferably) or formula. Increase the amount gradually to $2\frac{1}{2}$ to 3 tablespoons twice a day. In addition, 6 breastfeedings are recommended in the fourth month, and 5 to 6 in the fifth. Your infant should suckle about 10 to 20 minutes at each breast. If your baby is on formula, five 5 to 8 ounce feedings daily is required in month 4, and five 6 to 8 ounce feedings in month 5.

You can begin with any cereal, but most paediatricians prefer iron-fortified rice cereals as baby's first solid, since it is the cereal most unlikely to cause an allergic reaction. After that, introduce barley, oatmeal, wheat, or high-protein cereal one at a time over five-day intervals so that an allergic reaction to a specific cereal can be spotted, and the offending food stricken from your baby's diet.

During month 4, the cereal mixes, which you have prepared at first with a consistency only slightly less than that of breast milk or formula, is gradually thickened. By month 5, your baby is ready for the smooth, creamy texture of strained fruits and vegetables. You can use commercial baby foods, or you can prepare them yourself with a whirr of the blender from some of the cooked fruits and vegetables on our Eating Plan for Brighter Kids. *"A baby's food should not be seasoned with salt or vinegar"*, warns Boston Children's Hospital (emphasis theirs); and on our Basic Eating Plan, there's not a grain of sugar, and no salt or extremely small amounts that can be eliminated. Actually, most of the solid food for your baby from months 4 to 12 can be derived from that Plan.

Months 6 to 8. In the sixth month, for most breast-fed babies, bottle-fed formula is introduced and, for most babies, strained foods give way gradually to finely mashed ('junior-texture') foods. Should you delay this textural upgrading by a month or two, your baby may attempt to stay at the strained-food level even longer, lengthening the time a baby normally takes to eat regular family-textured foods (about 10 months to one year). A baby that has become accustomed to finely mashed foods in the sixth month, happily begins the transition to minced foods in the seventh.

During months 6 to 8, Dr. Minear recommends each day iron-enriched formula, cereal, vegetables, and fruit. He prefers that you serve your baby *"five meals a day and limit each serving of a solid to four tablespoons"* (emphasis his). Dr. Minear bases his five-meal preference essentially on "studies [that] have demonstrated . . . nutrients are best utilized . . . in the body in small amounts, rather than in large, infrequent servings". (Some paediatricians favour demand feedings up to seven months; others approve of starting infants on three meals a day in the sixth month. Your paediatrician should be your guide).

In the sixth month, your baby's food horizon is broadening. Now the menu of finely mashed fruits and vegetables, according to Dr. Spock, can include pineapples, string beans, squash (marrow), onions, asparagus, chard, and tomatoes. Many paediatricians add finely mashed macaroni, spaghetti, and noodles to that list. Soft ripe bananas, fork-mashed, get a nod of approval from Boston Children's Hospital.

But warning signs are up: avoid broccoli, cauliflower, cabbage, and sweet potatoes, warns Dr. Spock. Dr Minear tells you to eliminate onions and cucumbers. Nutritionist Miriam Erick, who specializes in developing intelligent eating techniques for mother and child, forbids coro, beans, and plain yoghurt. All nutrition scientists agree that infants' intestines, unlike older kids', are vulnerable to toxic spores that may appear in some honeys; so honey and foods containing it are outlawed for children under the age of 1.

Around the seventh month, your baby enjoys the first tastes of finely minced food, as chicken, lamb, liver, veal, and pork replace some of the cereal. Potatoes and pasta, finely minced, are also a delightful new experience. This is teething time, and hard toast and crackers help sooth the discomfort.

Perhaps the greatest joy of your infant's adventures in eating comes between the seventh and tenth months when finger foods are encountered. These small pieces of food that challenge the baby's growing ability to pick up things with thumb and forefinger. Gastronomically, they range from the soft baby-sized bits of cheese, ripe fresh fruits (peeled and seed-free), and steamed vegetables (no ends, strings and peels) to tofu cubes, mini-meatballs, and tiny slices of boneless and skinless tenderly cooked chicken and fish. Fun for infants, who treat these bright-hued morsels as toys—edible toys—they stir your child's brain, and are part of the food-stimulation mechanism of brain growth that began when you first took your baby to your breast.

Months 8 to 10. Dr. Minear's daily eating plan for this period calls for iron-fortified formula, juice, vegetables, fruits, meats, fish, yoghurt, cheese, cooked dried beans, peanut butter, and egg yolk. Egg yolk is an excellent source of brain-needed cholesterol. But egg whites, which may be allergens to some infants up to 10 months, are banned; as are egg-white-containing foods such as ice cream.

In the eighth month, your child is learning how to drink from a cup. Whole milk, not skimmed milk, replaces some of the formula. Mild spices delight the palate; and by the ninth month, the texture of chopped foods adds a new joy. If your child has been demand-fed up to the seventh month, the regime of three meals a day and snacks, begun then, has become fairly routine. You're delighted with the progress your baby is making toward eating family foods with the whole family.

Months 10 to 12. On Dr. Minear's eating plan, your baby is still on iron-fortified formula; but there's less of it. To that is added each day cereal, bread, fruit, vegetables, plain yoghurt, 1 whole egg; peanut butter, cooked dried beans, meat, fish, chicken, and fruit juice.

By the end of the twelfth month, you baby has been fed, Dr. Minear says, "the sort of food a baby needs to enhance . . . maximum brain growth in the first year of life". And for the years to come? At the age of 1, your baby has been weaned, and has taken a place at the family table, sharing the family's food. But how can you meet adult's needs and children's need with the same menu plan? How can you feed grown-ups right and your kids' bright with the same meals?

The answer, which follows, comes from the food/ brightness revolution in the kitchen.

PART IV

The Nutrition/Brightness Revolution in the Kitchen: The Eating Plan for Brighter Kids

CHAPTER 10

SELECTING YOUR KIDS' FOODS

The 181 Worst Foods for Your Kids' Brains; The 265 Best Foods for Your Kids' Brains

This part of the book is your operating manual for our Eating Plan for Brighter Kids. It tells you precisely what to do to feed your kids to brightness.

It starts in this chapter, with a group of foods to eliminate from your kitchen, and a group of foods to put on your 'must' list. Then, in subsequent chapters, it provides you with instructions for:

- setting up an easily do-able menu plan for brightness

- getting rid of the junk-food habit in an utterly different and delicious way

- learning how to create a four-star menu with our new 'bright cuisine'

- eating right to feed your kids bright during pregnancy and breastfeeding

- serving your kids the brightest foods from the age of 1 to adolescence

- selecting the right vitamin/mineral supplements for yourself during preconception, pregnancy, and breast-feeding; and for your kids, starting at the age of 2

The remarkable thing about this Eating Plan for Brighter Kids is that it's a single healthful programme for the whole family, simply modified for your special needs and your kids'.

What the 'Worst' and 'Best' Food Lists Are All About

A junk food is vitamin/mineral-impoverished, providing little support for kids' (and adults') bodies and brains. It's also rife with harmful ingredients that attack the body/brain and to which kids are especially vulnerable. These are sugar, salt and other sodium compounds, saturated fats, chemical colourings, flavourings, preservatives, stimulants, processing ingredients, and other additives.

A junk food is, for example, this mix: sugar (sucrose), non-fat milk solids, corn syrup solids, cream, whole milk, guar gum, emulsifier, carrageenan, salt, imitation vanilla powder, sodium alginate, cellulose gum, dextrose, and colourings. Recognize it? It's a 'milk shake' served in fast-food shops, and, unfortunately, still in many school canteens.

But some natural foods are as bad as junk foods — robbing children's brains of nutrients, impeding the brain's functions, and sometimes actually destroying the brain's tissues. They could make your kids hyperactive or slow learners; turn them into Jekyll and Hydes; slash their I.Q.'s; dull their brains; and produce a startling catalogue of mental, emotional, behavioural, and learning problems.

The most harmful of natural foods, and the most harmful of junk foods, have here been assembled for the first time in the 181 Worst Foods for Your Kids' Brains. Take the list into your kitchen, and if any of the items are on your shelves or in your fridge (they are), get rid of them today and never trundle them to the check-out counter again.

Instead, from now on make your food selection mainly from the 265 Best Foods for Your Kids' Brains. Fresh foods with the highest of nutrient contents, and a sprinkling of processed foods of exceptional value, they provide the soundest foundation for the health of your kids' brains and for the general health of the whole family. They're familiar foods, many are longtime favourites—*and* there's no need to go out of your way to get them. It seems unbelievable, but it's true: the road to your children's brightness begins in the supermarket.

One final incentive for making the switch from the worst foods to the best foods for your kids' brains: foods work on kids' brains fast. You could see results in just a few weeks. Or sooner.

The 181 Worst Foods for Your Kids' Brains

This is your guide to what foods to pass by as you wheel your cart from department to department in your supermarket. These foods should be eliminated on adults' as well as children's diets because, as a group, they are high in sugar and salt, contain excessive amounts of cholesterol and fats—all associated by nutrition scientists with adult degenerative diseases such as heart attack, diabetes, and cancer. All the products listed here are 'commercial'. **Asterisked (*) items** are foods that inhibit the action of some vitamins and minerals in the body/brain; but they can be used on a fully supplemented diet. For specific lists of foods that may trigger hyperactivity, brain allergens and brain dullness in some children, see Chapters 2, 3, and 5 respectively. A list of high-fibre foods, which when consumed in excess may harm some children's brains, is found in Chapter 7.

Baked Goods

Bagels	Gluten bread
Baking powder*	Pastries
Baking soda*	Pies
Brioches	Pumpernickel
Brownies	Rolls
Cakes and crackers	Rye bread

Biscuits
Corn bread
Croissants
Dietetic bread
Doughnuts

Salt sticks
Swedish crispbreads
Sweet rolls
White bread
Rusks

Beverages

Alcoholic beverages
Chocolate milk
Cocoa
Coffee
Diet drinks
Fruit-type drinks

Instant drinks
Soft drinks
    including cola drinks
Tea (including most herb
    teas)

Breakfast Foods

Bacon
Muesli
Ham

High-sugar breakfast
    cereals
Sausages

Canned, Frozen, and Instant Foods

Baking mixes
Stock cubes
Canned made-up
  dishes
Canned fruits
Canned juices
Canned soups
Canned vegetables
Dessert mixes

Frozen baked foods
Frozen prepared foods
  and meals
Frozen uncooked foods
Instant Breakfast mixes
Powdered drink mixes
Prepared stuffings
Sauce mixes

(Exceptions in this category are canned salt-,
sugar- and additives-free products when used on
a fully supplemented diet.)

Condiments, Sauces, Salad Dressings

Chilli sauce
Chutney
Horseradish
Ketchup
Mayonnaise
Prepared mustards

Salad dressings,
    packaged and bottled
Soy and other Oriental
    sauces
Steak sauces
Tabasco

Cooked Take-Aways

Barbecued poultry
French fries
Fried chicken
Fried fish
Hamburgers
Rotisseried chicken

Dairy Products

Coffee whiteners
Dessert whips, synthetic
Egg whites*
Flavoured yoghurts
High-fat cheeses (such as Brie, Gruyère and Gorgonzola)
Processed cheeses

Delicatessen

Bologna
Coleslaw
Fish salads
Frankfurters
German-type wursts (including liverwurst)
Italian-type cold cuts (including prosciutto)
Luncheon meat
Meat salads
Olives
Pastrami
Pickled vegetables (including 'pickles')
Salami
Sauerkraut
Vegetable salads

Desserts

Sweets
Chocolate
Custards
Flavoured gelatine
Fruit toppings
Ice cream
Ice milk
Ices
Jams
Jellies
Junket desserts
Mousses
Puddings
Sorbets
Syrups

Fats and Oils

Artificially coloured butter (except if coloured with beta-carotene, which is beneficial)
Coconut oil
Hardened white vegetable shortenings (hydrogenated vegetable fats)
Margarine (with additives)
Lard and other animal fats
Palm oil

Fish

Caviar and other roes
Fillets, preserved in brine and/or artificially coloured
Fish, raw*
Crab sticks

Smoked fish (including Scotch salmon, Nova Scotia salmon, Norwegian salmon, finnan haddock)

Meats and Poultry

Capon
Duck
Fatty cuts of meat
Goose
Kidneys

Lungs
Roasting chicken
Self-basting poultry
Sweetbreads

Nuts and Vegetables

Almonds*
Avocados*
Beetroot, raw*
Cabbage, raw
Cassava*
Cauliflower*
Coconut
Corn and corn products* (except corn oil)
Horseradish*

Kale*
Mustard greens
Pinenuts
Rape
Swede*
Soya beans and soya bean products*
Spinach, raw*
Turnips, raw*
Vegetable greens, raw*
Watercress*

Snacks

Cheese puffs and similar snack items
Cream filled baked goods
Dips
Muesli
Peanuts

Popcorn
Potato crisps
Pretzels
Salted nuts
Seeds*
Snack-type fruit pies
Walnuts

Sugars and Sugar Substitutes

Aspartame
Beet Sugar
Blackstrap molasses
Brown sugar

Invert sugar
Mannitol
Maple syrup
NutraSweet

Cane sugar
Corn syrup
Dextrins
Fructose
Glucose
HFCS (high fructose
  corn syrup)
Honey, processed; or
  any for kids under
  the age of 1

Pancake syrups
Raw sugar
Saccharin
Sorbitol
Sucrose (table sugar)
Turbinado sugar
Xylitol

The 265 Best Foods for Your Kids' Brains

These are the foods with the highest obtainable nutrient content. The best possible foods for meeting the needs of your kids' bodies and brains, they're also the best possible foods for adult health needs. As a group, they're low in saturated fats and cholesterol, contain no added sugar and salt, and supply the right amount of fibre—all factors in warding off nutrition-related diseases. (The higher optimal amounts of fats and cholesterol needed by children from conception to at least ages 3 to 5 are provided for in our Eating Plan for Brighter Kids by menu planning).

The foods are arranged here in Food Groups, not the traditional four or five, but an easier-to-use eleven—one major result of the nutrition revolution in the kitchen. By selecting servings from each food group you can obtain the best possible nutritional mix for your children and the adults in your family. All foods are natural and fresh by modern standards, with the exceptions of a few acceptable processed foods. **Asterisked (*) items are** permitted only on a fully supplemented diet.

ANIMAL FOODS/EGGS

Eggs

Fish (Fish oils—an oil is a liquid fat—are polyunsaturated, the type of oil that fights nutrition-related diseases such as heart attack, diabetes, and cancer.)

Low Fat

Scallop	Perch
Cod	Pike
Plaice	Pollack
Grey mullet	Sea bass
Haddock	Skate
Hake	Sole

Moderate Fat

Bass (all varieties except sea bass)	Sea trout
	Salmon, pink
Mackerel	Smelt
Carp	Sturgeon
Halibut	Swordfish
Herring	Trout, fresh water
Monkfish	Tuna
Sea bream	Whiting

Meat*

(These are lean cuts. The fats are saturated, the type associated with nutrient-related diseases. Excess should be avoided. Even in small quantities saturated fats may not be metabolized properly without full vitamin/mineral supplementation. Chemical-free meat is recommended.)

Beef

Chuck steak	Roast beef (rolled)
Fillet steak	Rump
Stewing steak	Sirloin steak
Flank steak	T-bone steak
Porterhouse	

Lamb (leanest cuts)

Leg	Shoulder chops
Loin chops and other loin cuts	Rib chops

Pork (leanest cuts)
Fresh ham
Pork, cooked shoulder

Rabbit

Veal (leanest cuts)

Leg	Round
Loin chops and other loin cuts	Rump
	Shoulder chops

Venison

Poultry

Chicken	Squab (young pigeon)
Frying, light or dark meat	Turkey
Guinea fowl	Young, light or dark meat
Pheasant	
Quail	

Seafood

Crab	Mussels
Clams	Oysters
Crayfish	Scallops
Lobster	Shrimp

Food Group 2

MILK/YOGHURT/CHEESE

Milk (Buttermilk, non-fat, and skimmed for adults and adolescents; whole milk for pregnant and nursing mothers, and children up to the age of 5, at least)

Buttermilk	Skimmed milk
Dried milk	Whole dried milk
Non-fat dried milk	
Whole milk	

Yoghurt (see **Milk**)
Plain low-fat yoghurt
Plain whole-milk yoghurt

Cheese (non-processed)

Cottage cheese
Cheddar cheese
Mozzarella

Parmesan
Ricotta

Food Group 3

GRAINS

Barley
Millet
Old-fashioned rolled
  oats
Wheatgerm

Rice
Wheat flakes
Whole kasha (buckwheat)
Wild rice

Food Group 4

BREAD/CRACKERS/INGREDIENTS

Arrowroot flour
Baking soda*
Buckwheat flour
Cornflour
Baking powder, without
  aluminium*
Dried yeast
Pasta (preferably made
  from flour and water, no
  salt or other additives,
  Neapolitan style, like
  spaghetti, macaroni,
  and linguine)

Rye flour
Stone-ground wholemeal
  flour
Unbleached flour
Wholemeal pastry flour

Food Group 5

PULSES/NUTS/SEEDS

All nuts (especially
  walnuts, but
  almonds,* and
  peanuts* only on a
  fully supplemented
  diet)
All nut butters, see
  previous listing

Dried beans
Dried peas (including split
  peas and chickpeas)
Lentils
Sesame seeds
Sunflower seeds
Tofu (bean curd)*

81

VITAMIN-C FRUITS/VEGETABLES

Fruits

Black cherry
concentrate
Cantaloupe
Grapefruit
Guava
Honeydew melon
Juices (fresh; frozen
only on a fully
supplemented diet)
Limes
Mango
Orange
Papaya
Lemons
Pineapple
Strawberries
Tangerines

Vegetables

Broccoli
Cauliflower*
Green pepper
Parsnips
Peas
Mange tout
Potatoes
Rhubarb
Sprouts
Marrow (summer/winter)
Sweet potatoes
Sweet red pepper
Tomatoes†
Tomato juice†
Tomato paste†
Tomato purée†
Vegetable juices†
Courgettes

† *Canned, only with no salt added, on a fully
supplemented diet.*

Food Group 7

DARK GREEN VEGETABLES

Asparagus
Broccoli
Brussels sprouts*
Cabbage (cooked)
Chard
Chicory
Chinese cabbage
Endive
Dark leafy lettuce
Radiccio
Spring onions
Spinach (cooked)
Turnip (cooked)
Watercress*

Food Group 8

OTHER FRUITS/VEGETABLES

Fruits

Apples
Apricots
Bananas
Blueberries
Cherries
Cranberries
Dates
Figs
Grapes

Juices (fresh; frozen only
   on a fully supplemented
   diet)
Nectarines
Peaches
Pears
Plums
Prunes
Raisins
Raspberries

Vegetables

Artichoke
Bamboo shoots
Beetroot (cooked)
Carrots
Celery
Corn*
Corn for popping*
Cucumber

Aubergine
Green beans
Mushrooms
Okra
Onions
Pumpkin
Radishes
Yams

Food Group 9

FATS

Cold-pressed vegetable oils

Corn oil
Cottonseed oil
Peanut oil
Safflower oil
Sesame oil (not
   Oriental variety)

Soya bean oil
Sunflower oil
Virgin olive oil
Walnut oil

Butter, unsalted

(natural, or coloured
only with beta-carotene,
   which is beneficial)

SWEETS

Carob powder and
chips (unsweetened)
Date powder
Dried fruits
(unprocessed)
Fruit juices (fresh;
frozen only on a fully
supplemented diet)
Honey (uncooked,
unfiltered; not for
children under the
age of 1)

Nuts (raw), see under
"All nuts" in *Food
Group 5*
Nut pastes (no sugar or
salt added), see
previous listing
Sugar cane
Sweet herbs (aniseed,
marjoram, oregano,
coriander, ginger, mace,
sweet paprika)

Food Group 11

HERBS/SPICES/CONDIMENTS/FLAVOURINGS

Regarded until recently by conventional medical
science as non-nutritive, herbs and spices are
now known, thanks mainly to comprehensive
chemical analyses conducted by the U.S.
Department of Agriculture (USDA), to be replete
with essential vitamins and minerals. They may
also contribute substances that fight destructive
biochemicals (oxidants and their derivatives) that
attack all cells in the body, including the brain's.
We use both fresh and dried herbs.

Garlic is not only the most nutritionally potent
food in this group (it is a herb), but, used
judiciously, it can also be a culinary delight.
There's widening acceptance by conventional
doctors of this popular herb's preventive medical
properties.

Herbs/Spices

Allspice
Aniseed
Basil or sweet basil
Bay leaves
Caraway seeds
Cardamom seeds
Cayenne (red pepper)

Chervil
Chilli con carne
seasoning (no salt
added)
Chives
Cinnamon
Cloves

Coriander seeds
Cumin
Curry powder (no salt added)
Dill
Fennel seeds
Garlic
Ginger
Juniper berries
Mace
Marjoram
Mustard seeds
Nutmeg
Onion powder (not onion salt)
Oregano
Parsley
Pickling spices (no salt added)
Poppy seeds
Rosemary
Sage
Savory
Shallots
Tarragon
Thyme
Watercress

Condiments/Flavourings

Apple cider vinegar
Balsamic vinegar
Grain coffee (also called cereal beverage; not a coffee, but has a coffee-like flavour as an adult drink; as used as a flavouring in my recipes, it does not taste like coffee)
Low sodium vegetable seasoning
Pure vanilla extract
Reduced-sodium soy sauce
Vanilla pod
Wine vinegar

CHAPTER 11

PROBLEM-FREE MEALS FOR BRIGHTER KIDS

The Basic All-Family Menu Plan

The Basic All-Family Menu Plan is a model. Use it as-is, or spin off on your own variations by replacing any food you don't want to use with one of the foods from the same Food Group listed in the '365 Best Foods' listed on page 79. You can, for example, replace 'orange sections', a member of Food Group 6, Vitamin-C Fruits/Vegetables, with any of thirteen different fruits. This simple replacement technique helps you create an almost endless variety of menus. The Basic All-Family Menu Plan is an exciting, never boring healthful eating programme.

But if you meet wistful resistance from the junk-food lovers among you—including yourself—go to the next chapter and learn how to break the junk-food habit by including any of more than sixty 'junk foods' in the Basic All-Family Menu Plan. But the wonderful thing about these junk foods is that they taste like junk foods, they look like junk foods, they're named like junk foods, but they're not junk foods at all. They're healthful 'junk food' clones.

And if you long for that four-star gourmet touch—and we think it's wonderful if you do, because what a gift you'll be giving your kids by introducing them to the joys of the great tastes of good, healthful food—go to page 144 and learn how you can make our new 'Bright Cuisine' replacements on the Basic Menus.

The Basic All-Family Menu Plan, and its healthful 'junk-food' and Bright Cuisine variants, are easily adapted to your special needs during pregnancy and breastfeeding, and the needs to your kids form infancy to adolescence. Find out how to do it in Chapters 8 and 9, in Chapter 13, the bright supplements, and in the notes that follow recipes.

When should you start your family on the Basic All-Family Menu Plan?

Tomorrow. At breakfast.

The Basic All-Family Menu Plan

Before you begin, keep these notes in mind:

- The term *homemade* in the following menus means your own recipe prepared with minimum salt and no sugar.
- For an after-meal drink, for adults only, grain coffee (also called cereal beverage) is a caffeine-free coffee taste-alike. But it's not for kids; you don't want them to get used to the taste of coffee. Water is a great drink; many of us have forgotten how good it is.
- Oil and vinegar dressing is made with one part any vinegar and two parts vegetable oil.
- Butter or margarine for kids? Polyunsaturated margarine is lower in saturated fats, higher in polyunsaturated fats, and contains no cholesterol—all of which contributes to preventing cardiovascular problems and heart attack. This is fine for adults and children over the age of 5. But children under that age need cholesterol for the growth and functioning of the nervous system and the I.Q.-related glial-cell complex in the brain; and butter is an excellent source of cholesterol. We compromise by using a butter-margarine blend. Boston Children's Hospital advises that instead of purchasing a commercial combination, it's "easy and more economical to soften a packet of each and blend them together at home". Sweet butter (unsalted) without artificial colouring (except beta-carotene, which is beneficial) is the best of the butters; and margarine should be free of additives (except beta-carotene). Switching your over-age-5 children to margarine may be beneficial. There is no difference in calories between butter and regular margarine; but 'diet margarine', which contains more water, is less caloric.
- Do remember that this Basic All-Family Menu Plan is just that—the *base* for getting started—on which you can build your own exciting menus which include 'junk-food' clones and gourmet Bright Cuisine dishes.

Day 1

BREAKFAST

180 ml/6 fl oz low-fat plain yoghurt, mixed with fresh orange
   sections or 90 g/3 oz berries in season.
1 scrambled egg, prepared with:
   - 5 ml/1 tsp unsalted butter/margarine blend
   - pinch each curry powder and dried tarragon leaves,
     crushed
2 slices wholemeal bread
15 ml/1 tbsp unsweetened jam
250 ml/8 fl oz skimmed milk

LUNCH

250 ml/8 fl oz homemade tomato soup *or* low-sodium tomato
   juice served with homemade unsalted popcorn
1 tuna salad sandwich, prepared with:
   - 90 g/ 3 oz canned tuna packed in water
   - 15 ml/1 tbsp each chopped onion and celery
   - 10 ml/2 tsp fresh lemon juice
   - 5 ml/1 tsp olive oil
   - 2 slices wholemeal bread
1 fresh pear *or* apple

DINNER

$\frac{1}{4}$ small chicken, skinned, grilled or roasted, rubbed all
   over with
5 ml/1 tsp oil, and sprinkled with:
   - good pinch each mild paprika and onion powder
   - 1-2 ml/$\frac{1}{4}$ tsp dried sage leaves
   - pinch salt (optional)
1 medium baked yam or sweet potato
90 g/3 oz steamed broccoli, sprinkled with fresh lemon juice
1 small sliced tomato, surrounded with:
   - julienned green pepper
   - shredded carrot
   - radish roses
   - 15 ml/1 tbsp oil and vinegar dressing
90 g/3 oz fresh pineapple cubes, or canned crushed pineapple packed in unsweetened pineapple juice
250 ml/8 fl oz skimmed milk

Day 2

BREAKFAST

150 g/ 5 oz of grapefruit and orange sections, sweetened with:
- 5 ml/1 tsp honey dissolved in
- 30 ml/2 tbsp unsweetened apple juice

90 g/3 oz hot oatmeal seasoned with:
- pinch salt
- good pinch ground cinnamon
- 5 ml/1 tsp honey

2 slices wholemeal bread
5 ml/1 tsp unsalted butter/margarine blend
15 ml/1 tbsp unsweetened jam or unsweetened fruit butter
250 ml/8 fl oz skimmed milk

LUNCH

250 ml/8 fl oz homemade mushroom and barley soup
1 sliced chicken or turkey sandwich, prepared with:
- 2 slices wholemeal bread
- spread composed of 2.5 ml/$\frac{1}{2}$ tsp each tomato purée, olive oil, and prepared Dijon mustard
- 60 g/2 oz sliced chicken or turkey (do not use chicken or turkey roll)

1 medium tomato, sliced, topped with crisp alfalfa sprouts
90 g/3 oz homemade apple sauce sweetened with honey
250 ml/8 fl oz skimmed milk

DINNER

90 g/3 oz grilled veal patty, or sliced flank steak seasoned with herbs and spices
180 g/6 oz spaghetti or macaroni with homemade tomato sauce or salt/sugar-free commercial sauce, sprinkled with:
- finely chopped fresh herbs
- 2.5 ml/½ tsp freshly grated Parmesan cheese
  90 g/3 oz steamed green beans, sprinkled with:
- freshly grated nutmeg
- lemon juice

¼ small canteloupe, 90 g/3 oz fresh berries in season, 40 g/1 ½ oz raisin-nut mix
250 ml/8 fl oz skimmed milk

Day 3

BREAKFAST

90 g/ 3 oz sweet fruit compote, topped with:
- 15 ml/ 1 tbsp low-fat cottage cheese, and
- 30 ml/2 tbsp undiluted evaporated skimmed milk (it's sweet tasting and good)

1 shredded wheat biscuit, sprinkled with 15 ml/1 tbsp wheatgerm
250 ml/8 fl oz skimmed milk
1 slice wholemeal bread
2.5 ml/$\frac{1}{2}$ tsp unsalted butter/margarine blend
5-10 ml/1-2 tsp unsweetened jam

LUNCH

250 ml/8 fl oz low-sodium V-8 tomato juice
1 serving *Oriental Sauté*, prepared in wok or non-stick pan with:
- 10 ml/2 tsp hot peanut oil
- 275 g/9 oz combined thinly sliced spring onion, red or green pepper, mange tout, and broccoli florets
- 90 g/3 oz cubed tofu (bean curd) dried on kitchen paper
- 5 ml/1 tsp reduced-sodium soy sauce
- 30–45 ml/2-3 tbsp homemade chicken stock, or stock made with low-sodium vegetable seasoning

90 g/3 oz cooked brown rice
12 g/4 $\frac{1}{2}$ oz cubed fresh pineapple, *or* unsweetened pineapple chunks topped with 15 ml/1 tbsp unsalted peanut butter
250 ml/8 fl oz skimmed milk

DINNER

90 g/3 oz baked fresh fillet of cod *or* plaice, prepared with:
- 7.5 ml/1 $\frac{1}{2}$ tsp unsalted butter/margarine blend
  5 ml/ 1 tsp finely chopped fresh dill or parsley
- pinch salt

90 g/3 oz steamed fresh peas
1 medium baked potato, split and topped with:
- 15 ml/1 tbsp low-fat plain yoghurt

- 15 ml/1 tbsp chopped chives
1 slice wholemeal bread
2.5 ml/ ½ tsp unsalted butter/margarine blend
120 ml/ 4 ½ oz mixed salad, prepared with:
- 40 g/ 1 ½ oz each thinly sliced cucumber, or courgette, carrot, and mushrooms
- 15 ml/1 tbsp finely chopped onion, *or* spring onion, coarsely chopped
- 15 ml/1 tbsp oil and vinegar dressing
  1 medium banana, sliced and quickly sautéed in non-stick pan with:
- 5 ml/1 tsp unsalted butter/margarine blend
  1.25 ml/¼ tsp each ground ginger and cinnamon
- 5 ml/1 tsp fresh lemon juice (squeezed over cooked banana)

Day 4

BREAKFAST

1 whole orange, *or* 90 g/3 oz berries in season
90 g/3 oz fine oatmeal prepared with:
- 10 ml/ 2 tsp unprocessed bran
- pinch each ground cinnamon and cardamom
- 10 ml/ 2 tsp honey
2 slices wholemeal bread
5 ml/1 tsp unslated butter/margarine blend
15 ml/1 tbsp unsweetened jam or jelly
250 ml/8 fl oz skimmed milk

LUNCH

250 ml/8 fl oz homemade lentil soup
1 roast beef sandwich, prepared with:
- 90 g/ 3 oz lean roast beef
- 2 slices wholemeal bread
- spread composed of 2.5 ml/ ½ tsp each tomato purée, olive oil and prepared Dijon mustard
- freshly ground pepper (optional)
125 ml/ 4 fl oz homemade apple sauce sweetened with honey, *or* 40 g/ 1 ½ oz dried fruit, without preservatives
250 ml/ 8 fl oz skimmed milk

DINNER

2 small chicken legs (skinned) *or* 125 g/ 4 oz boned and skinned chicken breast, first lightly browned in 7.5 ml/ 1 ½ tsp corn oil, then sautéed with:
- 2.5 ml/ ½ tsp finely chopped garlic
- 15 ml/ 1 tbsp finely chopped shallot
- 30 ml/ 2 tbsp coarsely chopped green or red pepper
- 1 coarsely chopped tomato
- 2 pinches salt

    then cooked, covered, over low heat until tender

90 g/ 3 oz steamed sliced carrots, sprinkled with pinch freshly grated nutmeg

90 ml/ 3 oz cooked brown rice, sprinkled with finely chopped fresh rosemary, dill or parsley

180 g/ 6 oz cut-up fresh fruit, *or* 40 g/ 1 ½ oz dried fruit, without preservatives

250 ml/ 8 fl oz skimmed milk

Day 5

BREAKFAST

½ grilled grapefruit, spooned before grilling with:
- 5 ml/ 1 tsp honey
- 30 ml/ 2 tbsp unsweetened apple juice

    3 wholemeal flour pancakes, prepared from scratch in non-stick pan lightly coated with oil, batter mixed with skimmed milk (or a mixture of half skimmed milk and half whole milk)

15 ml/1 tbsp unsweetened jam

250 ml/ 8 fl oz skimmed milk

LUNCH

250 ml/ 8 fl oz homemade chicken soup with noodles or rice

1 heated pitta bread pocket filled with layers of:
- 40g/ 1½ oz each cooked warm beans and warm brown rice
- 1 coarsely chopped tomato
- 1 coarsely chopped hard boiled egg, and sprinkled with:

- 15 ml/ 1 tbsp finely chopped fresh parsley, dill, or rosemary
- pinch salt
250 ml/ 8 fl oz skimmed milk

DINNER

250 ml/ 8 fl oz low-sodium V-8 *or* tomato juice
90 g/ 3 oz serving homemade beef or veal stew
90 g/ 3 oz cooked bulgur (cracked wheat), sprinkled with:
- 2.5 ml/ ½ tsp finely chopped shallot
- 5 ml/ 1 tsp finely chopped fresh parsley, dill or rosemary
90 g/ 3 oz steamed baby onions, seasoned with:
- 2.5 ml/ ½ tsp unsalted butter/margarine blend
- pinch each salt and freshly grated nutmeg
1 serving courgette salad, consisting of:
- 40 g/ 1½ oz each alfalfa sprouts, grated carrot and courgette
- julienne strips red pepper
- 15 ml/1 tbsp oil and vinegar dressing
¼ small canteloupe, *or* raisin-nut mix
250 ml/ 8 fl oz skimmed milk

Day 6

BREAKFAST

1 medium baked apple, prepared with:
- 30 ml/ 2 tbsp unsweetened pineapple or apple juice
- 5 ml/1 tsp honey (optional)
- 1.25 ml/ ¼ tsp ground cinnamon
- pinch ground ginger
1 open-faced cottage cheese sandwich, made with:
- 2 slices wholemeal bread
- 90 g/ 3 oz low-fat cottage cheese, sprinkled with
- 15 ml/ 1 tbsp wheatgerm
250 ml/ 8 fl oz skimmed milk

LUNCH

90 g/ 3 oz hamburger, prepared with:
- 2 slices wholemeal bread

- spread composed of 2.5 ml/ ½ tsp each tomato purée, olive oil, and prepared Dijon mustard
- thinly sliced onion

1 serving mixed vegetable salad, consisting of:
- 1 coarsely chopped tomato
- 1 small sliced cucumber
- 4 sliced radishes
- 15 ml/ 1 tbsp oil and vinegar dressing
- 2.5 ml/ 1 tsp freshly grated Parmesan cheese

90 g/ 3 oz fresh pineapple cubes, *or* canned crushed pineapple packed in unsweetened pineapple juice
250 ml/ 8 fl oz skimmed milk

DINNER

250 ml/ 8 fl oz homemade split pea soup, *or* low-sodium tomato juice
- 90 g/ 3 oz poached fresh salmon, *or* 5 fresh prawns, prepared with:
- 5 ml/ 1 tsp unsalted butter/margarine blend
- 1.25 ml/ ¼ tsp dried crushed tarragon leaves
- pinch each salt and pepper
- fresh lemon juice

90 g/3 oz mashed potatoes, prepared with
- 10 ml/ 2 tsp low-fat plain yoghurt
- 15 ml/ 1 tbsp chopped chives
- good pinch curry powder
- pinch each salt and pepper

90 g/ 3 oz steamed fresh mange tout, seasoned with:
- 2.5 ml/ ½ tsp unsalted butter/margarine blend
- good pinch freshly grated nutmeg
- 1.25 ml/ ½ tsp apple cider vinegar
- pinch each salt and pepper

1 fresh pear, *or* medium slice of watermelon
250 ml/ 8 fl oz skimmed milk

Day 7

BREAKFAST

90 g/ 3 oz stewed dried fruit compote (see Breakfast, DAY 3), *or* whole orange

1 omelette, prepared in non-stick pan with:
- 2.5 ml/ ½ tsp unsalted butter/margarine blend
- 1 beaten egg
make filling in pan with:
- 5 ml/ 1 tsp olive oil
- 30 g/ 1 oz each chopped green pepper, onion and tomato
- 1.25/ ¼ tsp crushed dried oregano leaves

2 slices wholemeal bread
250 ml/ 8 fl oz skimmed milk

LUNCH

250 ml/ 8 fl oz homemade gazpacho *or* tomato soup
1 sardine sandwich, prepared with:
- 90 g/ 3 oz sardines packed in water
- 15 ml/ 1 tbsp chopped spring onion or onion
- 5 ml/ 1 tsp fresh lemon juice
- 2 slices wholemeal bread
- spread composed of 5 ml/1 tsp softened unsalted butter/margarine blend, mixed with prepared Dijon mustard

1 medium banana
250 ml/ 8 fl oz skimmed milk

DINNER

½ guinea fowl (skinned), roasted
180g/ 6 oz cooked orzo (rice-shaped pasta) with homemade tomato sauce, sprinkled with:
- finely chopped fresh herbs
- 2.5 ml/½ tsp freshly grated Parmesan cheese 90 g/ 3 oz steamed green beans

chicory 'coleslaw' prepared with:
- 90 g/ 3 oz chicory, thinly sliced
- 40 g/ 1 ½ oz grated carrot
- 5 ml/1 tbsp finely chopped onion or spring onion
- pinch each salt and pepper
- 15 ml/ 1 tbsp oil and vinegar dressing, mixed with 30 ml/ 2 tbsp buttermilk

1 fresh peach or pear, *or* 40 g/ 1 ½ oz raisin-nut mix
250 ml/8 fl oz skimmed milk

Snacks
(especially for kids at mid afternoon)

If some of these snacks sound like junk foods, they are. But they're not . . . they're healthful junk-food clones.

Some of these require no recipes. For those that do, refer to the page reference in parentheses following the name of the snack.

Fresh fruit

Fresh vegetable, cut up

Dried fruit, without preservatives

Popcorn, plain

Popcorn (page 121)

Raisin-nut mix

Fruit Butter (page 112)

Soups (pages 120, 131 and 151)

Muesli, commercial, without sugar or preservatives

Milk shakes (pages 142 and 150)

Prunes

Fruit butters, commercial without sugar or preservatives

Plain rice crackers, spread with commercial unsweetened jam

Peanut butter

Peanut butter with plain yoghurt

CHAPTER 12

BREAKING YOUR FAMILY'S JUNK-FOOD HABIT

Healthy 'Junk-Food'

This may be the most important chapter in this book. If you and your husband can break the junk-food habit, you have a better chance for a healthful life. If your kids can break the junk-food habit, they have a better chance for a healthful life, *and* for a brighter life.

Yet it's not easy. The junk-food habit is all-pervasive. It's as natural to us as eating in and eating out. Almost all supermarket food is junk—read the labels. All fast-food and take-out food, even the sophisticated kind, are junk foods, although there are no labels to read. If there were, *The New York Times* commented editorially in 1986, "the result might be a healthy change in the nation's eating habits".

But labelling and cautionary advice have not made any dents in megabillion-dollar supermarket junk-food sales, and won't in the newer but already $ billion, and growing explosively, fast-food/take-out industry. When the plates are down, it's taste that counts—and, you can't get away from it, junk foods taste finger-lickin' good.

So what we're giving you and your kids to help start breaking the junk-food habit is healthful food that tastes like—and sometimes even looks like—junk food. Just imagine—

Healthful:

Beefburgers. Hamburger Buns. Chips. Ketchup. Bread. Copy Cat Chicken McNuggets.

Healthful:

Wonder-Ful Bread. Cuppa-Soup. Real Mayonnaise. Canned-type Tomato Soups.

Healthful:

Lasagne. Fish Fingers. Pizza. Tangy potato. Spaghetti sauce.

Healthful:

Lollipops. Fruit Jelly. Chewy Fruit Muesli Bars. Fruit Butter. Ice cream shakes. Popcorn.

How to Use Your Healthy 'Junk-Food' Recipes

It's simplicity itself. If you wish to replace a dish with a healthful 'junk-food' just look in the list of the clones that follows, and substitute any for a matching dish in the Basic All-Family Menu Plan. 'Matching' means appetizer for appetizer, first course for first course, dessert for dessert, and so forth.

Examples: For Breakfast, instead of shredded wheat, why not a healthful 'junk-food' Chewy Fruit Muesli Bar? For Lunch, instead of vegetable/egg-stuffed pitta, how about a healthful 'junk-food beefburger on a Hamburger Bun? For dinner, instead of poached salmon, wouldn't you like healthy Fish and Prawn Fingers? Some of them are so simple that you can teach your kids to make them. They're marked with a **K** for Kids.

There are two kinds of clones. One tastes more like real junk food than the other. (That's because some contain minute amounts of sugar, and some contain more fat than we ordinarily use.) These clones—still healthful by any standards—act as transitions (in-betweens) between real junk foods and our no-sugar, really low-fat clones.

Here's the trick: use the in-between clones first. Then, when your kids get used to them—it's easy, because they do resemble junk foods—introduce no-sugar, really low-fat clones. The tastes are so close to the in-betweens that your kids will get used to *them* fast. As a matter of fact, after a while your kids won't be able to tell the difference between the in-betweens and the real clones.

Then you can do one of two things: you can drop the in-between clones from your menu, or you can follow our suggestions at the end of each in-between 'junk-food' recipe, and convert it into a no-sugar, really low-fat 'junk-food' clone.

CHAPTER 13

VITAMINS AND MINERALS

The Bright Supplements for You and Your Kids

Processing, even of fresh food, has so diminished our food's natural supply of vitamins and minerals that even the best possible diet must be supplemented to reach optimal health levels for body and mind.

RDAs are Recommended Dietary Allowances set by government agencies to prevent the onset of vitamin/mineral-deprivation diseases. ODAs are Optimal Dietary Allowances, on the whole higher than RDAs, established by some medical nutrition scientists as necessary to help prevent pre-clinical symptoms of those diseases. All the supplements recommended—for preconception, for pregnancy and breast-feeding, and for kids from aged 2 to 12—are ODA formulations. These are not 'megadoses', extraordinary large quantities of vitamins/mineral, even though the therapeutic uses of megadoses have been helpful in treating many kinds of children's mental diseases.

Dr. Bernard Rimland has documented successes with numerous cases of autism (a disease that prevents a child from relating or communicating meaningfully with other human beings). Dr. Abram Hoffer, a Canadian Public Health Department official, and Dr. Henry Osmond, a New Jersey neuropsychiatric specialist, improved the condition of schizo-phrenics (victims of a disease characterized by delusions, hallucinations and a loss of a sense of reality). Dr. Henry Turkel, a Michigan paediatrician specializing in the treatment of retarded children, has reported significant reversals in retardation, even among children born with Down's disease (mongolism). Dr. Allan Cott has recorded major victories over a wide range of learning disabilities.

But megadoses must be prescribed and closely monitored by physicians with in-depth backgrounds in nutrition. Megadoses of vitamins/minerals could, for some children, be dangerous and even fatal. Dr. Earl L. Mindell, a leader in establishing safe and sensible levels of vitamin/mineral supplementation for mother and child, says, "I firmly believe [they] are as important as love . . . for the continuing vitality and happiness of your children in the years ahead".

A Pregnancy and Breastfeeding ODA Supplement

This insurance formula is the only one we know that provides at least pregnancy RDAs for all vitamins and minerals (except phosphorus, which is adequately supplied by our All-Family Menu Plan). Called Pre-Natal Formula, it contains ample amounts of iron, folic acid and calcium, vital for the health of mother and child during the crucial months of child bearing and breastfeeding. For optimal safety, Beta Carotene is the vitamin A source. Manufacturer's recommended dose is 3 tablets with breakfast and 3 with dinner.

6 tablets supply

A (Beta Carotene)	10,000 IU
B₁ (Thiamin HCl)	3.4 mg
B₂ (Riboflavin)	4 mg
Niacin	40 mg
Calcium Pantothenate	20 mg
B₆ (Pyridoxine HCl)	5 mg
B₁₂ (Cobalamin Concentrate)	16 mcg
Biotin	300 mcg
Folic Acid	800 mcg
C (Ascorbic Acid)	240 mg
D₃ (Cholecalciferol)	600 IU
E (d-alpha-Tocopheryl Acetate)	60 IU

6 tablets supply

K₁ (Phytonadione)	100 mcg
Calcium (Carbonate)	1,300 mg
Magnesium (Oxide)	450 mg
Iron (Ferrous Fumarate)	50 mg
Zinc (Gluconate)	25 mg
Manganese (Gluconate)	5 mg
Copper (Gluconate)	2 mg
Selenium (L-Selenomethionine)	200 mcg
Chromium (Chromium Acetate)	200 mcg
Molybdenum (Sodium Molybdate)	150 mcg
Silicon (Magnesium Trisilicate)	20 mg

NOTE: IU stands for International Units; mg for milligrams; mcg for micrograms.

A Non-Pregnancy ODA Supplement

This formulation belongs to a category of multi-vitamin/mineral combinations called 'insurance formulas'. An 'insurance formula', according to an expert on commercial nutrient supplements, Dr. Sheldon Hendler, "is one that contains at least the RDAs as well as upper limits of safe and adequate doses of all essential trace minerals, major minerals, and vitamins. Insurance formulas, at their best, strive for a balance of nutrients that seem optimal given present knowledge. They are designed to help prevent the premature onset of degenerative diseases".

	6 tablets supply
A (as Beta Carotene)	25,000 IU
(as Retinyl Palmitate)	5,000 IU
B$_1$ (Thiamin HCl)	10 mg
B$_2$ (Riboflavin)	10 mg
Niacin	100 mg
Calcium Pantothenate	50 mg
B$_6$ (Pyridoxine HCl)	50 mg
B$_{12}$ (Cobalamin Concentrate)	30 mcg
Folic Acid	400 mcg
Biotin	100 mcg
C (Ascorbic Acid)	1,000 mg
D$_3$ (Cholecalciferol)	400 IU
E (d-alpha-Tocopheryl Acetate)	400 IU
K$_1$ (Phytonadione)	100 mcg

	6 tablets supply
Choline (Bitartrate)	250 mg
Calcium (Carbonate)	1,000 mg
Magnesium (Oxide)	400 mg
Zinc (Gluconate)	30 mg
Iron (Ferrous Fumarate)	18 mg
Manganese (Gluconate)	10 mg
Copper (Gluconate)	3 mg
Selenium	200 mcg
Chromium	100 mcg
(as Chromium Acetate)	100 mcg
Iodine (Potassium Iodide)	150 mcg
Molybdenum (Sodium Molybdate)	150 mcg
Magnesium (Magnesium Trisilicate)	20 mg

An ODA Supplement for Your Kids

There are no specific numerical recommendations for supplementation between birth and the age of 2. An iron supplement is usually added to baby formulas and foods to meet the RDA, but supplementation is at the discretion of your nutritionally knowledgeable doctor. Dr. Lendon Smith, the renowned paediatrician, prescribes an early start to supplementation with "brewer's yeast and wheat germ [excellent sources of B-complex vitamins] mixed in old-fashioned peanut butter . . . and vitamin C as a concentrated powder". But he's vague as to when to start and how much to give.

That's as it should be, Kids between birth and the age of 2 change so rapidly, and their needs are so individual that no general supplementation formula is applicable. Consult a nutritionally trained and experienced physician.

Some insurance formulas for children contain selenium and chromium. Selenium not only fortifies your child's immune system and fights cancer, but is also an essential ingredient of glutathione peroxidase, a biochemical manufactured in your child's body that several studies have linked to I.Q. Chromium plays a vital role in the metabolism of glucose, the energy source for your child's brain.

This product contained no milk, wheat, yeast or soy protein which may produce allergic reaction in some children. It is also free of artificial flavours, colourings and preservatives. For optimal safety it contains iron in its elemental form and vitamin A as beta-carotene. Phosphorus and calcium, which do not appear in the formula, are adequately supplied by our All-Family Menu Plan adapted for kids. Always follow the manufacturer's recommended dose when using any supplement.

A (Beta Carotene)	10,000 IU
B_1 (Thiamin HCl)	1.5 mg
B_2 (Riboflavin)	1.7 mg
Niacin	20 mg
Calcium Pantothenate	10 mg
B_6 (Pyridoxine HCl)	2 mg

B$_{12}$ (Cobalamin Concentrate)	6 mcg
Folic Acid	400 mcg
Biotin	100 mcg
C (Ascorbic Acid)	240 mg
D$_1$ (Cholecalciferol)	200 IU
E (d-alpha-Tocopherol Acetate)	30 IU
K$_1$ (Phytonadione)	100 mcg
Magnesium (Chelate)	80 mg
Zinc (Chelate)	10 mg
Iron (Micronised Elemental)	18 mg
Manganese (Chelate)	5 mg
Copper (Chelate)	2 mg
Selenium (L-Selenomethionine)	150 mcg
Chromium (Chromium Acetate)	150 mcg
Iodine (Potassium Iodide)	150 mcg
Molybdenum (Sodium Molybdate)	150 mcg

NOTE: IU stands for International Units; mg for milligrams; mcg for micrograms.

PART V

The Magic of Cooking Bright

Before You Begin

We were in a supermarket in Tampa, Florida (food shops are our first destination wherever we go), and a woman wheeling a trolley packed higher than the rim with frozen TV dinners, ice creams, sugared breakfast cereals, and package after package of cakes and candies, stopped us and said:

"Saw you on TV, and let me tell you something. Nutrition is no good if it don't taste good."

She's right.

And that's what scientists, doctors, and nutritionists who tell you what you should eat forget. You *can't* eat it if it "don't taste good." And neither can your kids.

The magic of cooking bright *makes* it taste good, makes healthful but dull, blah, *ugh*-ly ingredients taste not just good, but great— and that's why it's magic. It's a magic that can be learned, and this cookery book shows you how.

If you haven't cooked before—*really* cooked— you have one of life's greatest experiences before you. It opens a world of infinite delights. Cooking is a creative joy that can turn anyone into an artist. Share that joy with your husband and your kids. For your spouse, as it is for you, it's a new adventure in living. For your kids, it's that and an exciting stimulant to the growth of new neurotransmitter pathways of learning in the brain. For the whole family, there's no more satisfying experience than eating together the food you've cooked together.

To put the magical taste into your dishes, begin by stocking up on those ingredients that are pure sorcery in the kitchen—herbs and spices (you'll find them listed under Food

105

Group 11, page 84). But that's just the start of your cooking wizardry as you learn by doing, recipe by recipe.

Shopping for the ingredients in these recipes is easy because you can find almost everything in your supermarket, including the herbs and spices, which are growing more popular every day. But there are a few items more readily available in health-food stores than elsewhere and here they are (including some for in-between 'junk-food' clones only):

Black cherry concentrate; blackstrap molasses, third extraction; baking powder, without aluminium; buckwheat flour; carob powder and chips, unsweetened; coconut, unsweetened; cold pressed oils; date powder (sometimes called date sugar); dried dates and apricots without preservatives; grain coffee; honey, uncooked, unfiltered; low-sodium vegetable seasoning; plain whole-milk yoghurt; sesame seeds, unhulled; smoked yeast (sometimes called bacon yeast); wheat flakes; whole kasha (buckwheat groats); and wholemeal pastry flour.

And some healthful hints:

When no specific oil is mentioned in a recipe, select any from Food Group 9, page 83. They're all among the most healthy.

Be sure to remove the skin from your poultry. More than 20 per cent of the chicken's fat—it's saturated to boot—lurks under the skin.

Don't use the skins of vegetables unless they're well scrubbed to help rid them of harmful additives. In Cooking Bright recipes, onions, shallots, garlic, fresh ginger, and turnip are peeled; carrots are peeled or well scrubbed; and courgette is well scrubbed but not peeled.

Wash and dry all meats, fish, chicken, vegetables and fruit *always*. That helps get rid of the dangerous chemical additives, and some of the pathogenic bacteria. After cutting, washing and drying any food, thoroughly wash your hands, your cutting board and any utensil touched by the food.

If you're using Cooking Bright recipes as a basis for baby foods for your under-1-year-old, eliminate honey and replace with concentrated fruit juice.

Don't use copper or aluminium cookware. They're anti-vitamin. Iron pots are fine though; they release much-needed iron into your food. Non-stick frying pans cut the need for fat; so use them, too.

To preserve the vitamin content in fruits and vegetables,

steam (or cook in as little water as possible), don't prepare them far ahead of cooking time, and don't let them soak too long in water (except dried beans and other legumes). Save your vitamin-rich cooking water for soups and stocks.

And some cooking tips:

Depending on the type of frying pan used (enamelled, cast iron, non-stick), cooking times and liquid remaining will differ. Cast iron frying pans which conduct heat rapidly and retain heat, will brown foods and cook them more rapidly than non-stick or enamelled frying pans.

Should you run out of Chicken Stock (page 112), or want to extend the stock you have on hand, use 5 ml/ 1 tsp low-sodium vegetable seasoning per 250 ml/ 8 fl oz boiling water. Taste will differ, but you'll like it.

It's not inconsistent to start with no-salt-added canned tomatoes and tomato juice, then add some salt. Here's why: most canned salt-added tomato products contribute 250 to 500 or more milligrams (mg.) sodium per serving. Adding just a pinch of salt to a no-salt-added canned tomato juice recipe serving four boosts sodium per serving by only about 90 to 180 mg., amounts more healthy for children and adults as well.

I use large eggs in all recipes calling for eggs.

To get the most out of Cooking Bright bread recipes, keep this in mind: the amount of flour is approximate because there is a wide variation in the ability of flour to absorb moisture. Should a recipe call for 400 - 500 g/ 14 oz - 1 lb, always start with the lesser amount. You can always *add* more flour but you can't *remove* what you've already put in. Too much flour will produce a dense, hard, untasty loaf. Rising time will vary depending upon humidity and air temperatures in *your* kitchen. Baking times vary slightly with the efficiency of *your* oven.

In Cooking Bright recipes, milk means *whole* milk and plain yoghurt means plain *whole* yoghurt. Use skimmed or low-fat varieties only when specified. No substitutions, please, for health and culinary reasons.

The Cooking Bright recipes that follow are Francine Prince originals. For the remainder of 'The Magic of Cooking Bright' she will be guiding you in their use as if she were giving you personal lessons.

Now enter the magic world of cooking bright . . .

The Magic Mixers: Recipes to Make All Recipes Taste Better

Following are nine mixers that could change your life in the kitchen. They're your gateway to expedience, flavour and economy; and they're so versatile, you'll discover many exciting new ways to use them.

I've included measurements for sample-size portions (enough for at least one recipe) of my dry mixers and Frozen Vegetable Mix so you can try them, if you like, before making up large batches.

Since developing these mixers, I've found I'm utterly lost without them. I store them on my shelf or in my freezer or refrigerator at all times for whipping up quick batches of cakes, spaghetti sauce, seasoned popcorn and many of our favourites.

Since my Magic Mixers significantly speed up the preparation of so many delightful dishes (you can cut preparation time by at least 50 per cent), you'll find it easy to prepare healthful and exciting dishes for your family every day.

BATTER AND CAKE MIX

For about 350 g/ 12 oz	For about 2.3 kg/5 ¼ lb	
250 g/8 oz	1.3 kg/2 ¾ lb	plain flour
75 g/2½ oz	450 g/15 oz	strong wholemeal flour
12.5 ml/2½ tsp	75 ml/5 Tbsp	baking powder
30 ml/2 Tbsp	50 g/1 ¾ oz	dried skimmed milk
Pinch	3.75 ml/ ¾ tsp	salt
2.5 ml/½ tsp	15 ml/ 1 tsp	ground cinnamon
30 ml/ 2 Tbsp	150 g/ 5 oz	sugar
30 ml/2 Tbsp	90 g/3 oz	date powder
30 ml/2 Tbsp	60 g/2 oz	wheatgerm

1. Sift the flours, baking powder, milk, salt and cinnamon into a large stockpot or bowl. Add the sugar and wheatgerm. Stir constantly, turning over the mixture many times, until well mixed.
2. To store, spoon into labelled containers leaving 5 cm/ 2 inches headspace. Before measuring, stir the mixture (do not shake), turning over the ingredients several times.

NOTE: this recipe may be prepared without sugar. For about 350 g/ 12 oz, eliminate sugar, increase date powder to 30 g/ 1 oz and the cinnamon measurement to 3.75 ml/ ¾ tsp. For about 2.3 kg/ 5 ¼ lb eliminate sugar, increase date powder measurement to 80 g/ 6 oz and cinnamon measurement to 15 ml/1 tbsp.

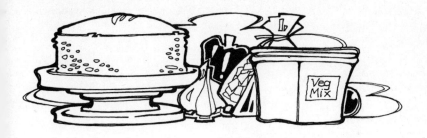

FROZEN VEGETABLE MIX

For about 500 g/1 lb	*For about 1.5 kg/3 lb*	
2	6	*medium carrots, peeled*
2	6	*medium onions, peeled*
1	3	*medium green pepper(s), seeded and cored*
2	6	*large celery stalks, ends trimmed*
3	9	*large cloves garlic, peeled*
1	3	*1 cm/½ inch/ slice(s) fresh root ginger, peeled*
15 g/½ oz	45 g/ 1½ oz	*fresh parsley leaves*

1. Cut the carrots, onions, green pepper and celery into 5 cm/ 2 inch lengths. Cut each garlic clove in half, and the ginger into squares. Fit a food processor with a steel blade. Arrange the cut vegetables in layers, starting with the carrots and ginger, then adding layers of celery, parsley, onion, garlic and green pepper. Coarse-chop by processing on/off 4 to 6 times. (If 1.5 kg/ 3 lb are being prepared, process in 3 batches.)
2. Transfer to polythene bags or freezerproof containers in 90 g/ 3 oz or 250 g/ 8 oz portions. Close tightly and freeze.
3. When ready to use, let stand at room temperature for 15 minutes, then break up. The mixture is now ready to use. Complete defrosting is not necessary.

SHAKE AND BAKE-ALIKE

For about 300 g/ 10 oz	For about 1 kg/ 2 lb	
45 g/ 1 ½ oz		toasted, unhulled sesame seeds
45 ml/ 3 tbsp		wheatgerm
50 g/ 2 oz	180 g/ 6 oz	fine toasted breadcrumbs
40 g/ 1 ⅓ oz	125 g/ 4 oz	stoneground yellow cornmeal
45 g/ 1 ½ oz	125 g/ 4 oz	each stoneground wholemeal flour and plain flour
30 g/ 1 oz	90 g/ 3oz	freshly grated Parmesan cheese
15 ml/ 1 Tbsp	45 ml/ 3 Tbsp	finely chopped lemon rind
5 ml/ 1 tsp	15 ml/ 1 tsp	ground ginger
2.5 ml/ ½ tsp	7.5 ml/1 ½ tsp	each dry mustard and ground cinnamon
25 ml/ 5 tsp	30 g/ 1 oz plus 15 ml/ 1 Tbsp	onion salt
Pinch	1.25 ml/ ¼ tsp	cayenne pepper
2.5 ml/ ½ tsp	7.5 ml/ ½ tsp	salt

1. Combine all the ingredients in a large bowl. Stir continually, turning over the mixture many times, until well mixed.
2. To store, spoon into labelled containers, leaving 5 cm/ 2 inches headspace. Before measuring, stir the mixture (do not shake), turning over the ingredients several times.

SEASONING MIX

For a little less than 45 ml/ 3 Tbsp	For a little less than 125 g/ 4 oz	
10 ml/ 2 tsp	30 ml/ 2 Tbsp	ground dried onion
5 ml/ 1 tsp	15 ml/ 1 Tbsp	ground dried garlic
15 ml/ 1 Tbsp	45 ml/ 3 Tbsp	low-sodium vegetable seasoning
5 ml/ 1 tsp	15 ml/ 1 Tbsp	dried yeast
2.5 ml/ ½ tsp	75 ml/ ½ tsp	onion powder
1.25 ml/ ¼ tsp	3.75 ml/ ¾ tsp	salt
5 ml/ 1 tsp	15 ml/ 1 Tbsp	dried dill
2.5 ml/ ½ tsp	7.5 ml/ 1 ½ tsp	dried parsley flakes
1.25 ml/ ¼ tsp	3.75 ml/ ¾ tsp	ground cinnamon
2.5 ml/ ½ tsp	7.5 ml/ 1 ½ tsp	dried sage

1. Combine all the ingredients in a small bowl, gently stirring to blend. Transfer to a jar. Store, tightly closed in a cool dry place.
2. Because the heavier ingredients tend to drift toward the bottom of the mix after standing a while, stir well before each use.

SPICY MIX

For about 37.5 ml/ 2 ½ Tbsp	For a little less than 80g/3 oz	
7.5 ml/ 1/1½ tsp	30 ml/ 2 Tbsp	onion powder
3.75 ml/ ¾ tsp	15 ml/ 1 Tbsp	dried parsley flakes
3.75 ml/ ¾ tsp	15 ml/ 1 Tbsp	dried rosemary, crushed
7.5 ml/ 1 ½ tsp	30 ml/ 2 Tbsp	dried oregano, crushed
3.75 ml/ ¾ tsp	15 ml/ 1 Tbsp	mild curry powder
2.5 ml/ ½ tsp	10 ml/ 2 tsp	ground ginger
1.25 ml/ ¼ tsp	5 ml/ 1 tsp	ground allspice
7.5 ml/ 1 ½ tsp	30 ml/ 2 Tbsp	chilli con carne seasoning (see Note)
1.25 ml/ ¼ tsp	5 ml/ 1 tsp	salt
1.25 ml/ ¼ tsp	5 ml/ 1tsp	ground cumin

1. Combine all ingredients in small bowl, gently stirring to blend. Transfer to jar. Store, tightly closed in cool dry place.
2. Because heavier ingredients tend to drift toward bottom of mix after standing a while, stir well before each use.

NOTE: Chilli con carne 'seasoning' contains no salt. Chilli con carne 'powder' contains an appreciable amount of salt. The 'seasoning' has a milder flavour.

FRUIT BUTTER—a sweetening staple

You don't have to sample this one, it's sweet-tooth proof.

250 g/ 8 oz dried dates (without preservatives added)
250 g/ 8 oz dried apricots (without preservatives added), well rinsed
150 g/ 5 oz raisins

5 cm/ 2 inch length vanilla pod, split
500 ml/ 16 fl oz unsweetened apple juice
5 ml/ 1 tsp ground cinnamon
30 ml/2 Tbsp frozen pineapple orange juice concentrate

1. Place all ingredients in heavy-based large saucepan. Bring to the boil. Reduce the heat to simmering, cover and simmer for 20 minutes, stirring from time to time. Remove from the heat and let stand, covered, until cooled. (Most of liquid will be absorbed.)
2. Using the food mill, purée one third of the mixture, reserving the solids. Store in airtight glass container for up to 3 weeks.

MAKES: about 625 g/ 1 ¼ lb purée; about 250 g/ 8 oz solids

SERVING SUGGESTIONS: serve as an infant fruit purée; it has far more flavour and nutrition than any commercial fruit purée.

Serve purée or solids as breakfast or dessert, plain, topped with ice-cold undiluted evaporated milk or mixed with desired amount of plain yoghurt.

'CANNED' CHICKEN STOCK

My chicken stock, a treasurehouse of nutrients and flavours, is used in many recipes. It's a lighter, quicker-cooking version of traditional chicken stock. Replete with flavourful essences of chicken, vegetables and herbs, it does wonders for soups, sauces and gravies. It's easy to make, simmering away happily by itself while you're busy with other chores.

1 chicken, including neck and gizzard, skinned and butterflied
1.5 litres/ 50 fl oz water
2 medium onion, coarsely chopped
2 carrots, peeled and thickly sliced
4 large garlic cloves, coarsely chopped
3 celery stalks, cut into chunks
6 large sprigs fresh parsley or dill or a combination of both
1 cm/ ½ inch slice fresh root ginger, peeled and chopped
40 g/ 1⅓ oz white turnip, peeled and sliced
125 g/ 4 oz fresh mushrooms, ends trimmed, rinsed dried and coarsely chopped
2.5 ml/ ½ tsp each dried thyme and sage

1. Lay the chicken, flesh side down, in large flameproof casserole. Add the remaining ingredients, except the thyme and sage. Slowly bring to a gentle boil. Skim the surface with large spoon, then add the thyme and sage. Cover and simmer for 2 hours, stirring from time to time.
2. With a slotted spoon remove the chicken. (Reserve for sandwiches, salads or main course.) Pour the stock and solids into a fine sieve. Press out the juices, then strain through muslin.
3. Transfer to freezeproof containers. Cover tightly and refrigerate overnight. Discard the fat that rises to the top. The clear, virtually fat-free stock is ready to use.

MAKES: about 1.3 litres/ 45 fl oz

STORING SUGGESTIONS: for a child's meal, or as an addition to any recipe calling for chicken stock, for quick access to 30 ml/ 2 Tbsp measures, fill each cube of large ice cube trays with 30 ml/2 Tbsp fat-skimmed stock; freeze. Remove the cubes and store in freezer bags for instant use.

NOTES: if you're stocked with Frozen Vegetable Mix (page xxx), substitute 350 g/ 12 oz of the mix for the onions, carrots, garlic, celery, parsley and ginger. Continue with the remaining recipe.

If you're preparing the recipe as written, vegetable chunks may be removed from the sieve before pressing out the juices in step 2, and reserved for a delicious meal for a baby. Strain the solids, or purée in a baby food grinder or food mill, or chop with a knife. Stock or plain yoghurt may be added to adjust the consistency. There should be about 250 ml/ 8 fl oz purée, which can be frozen and used as needed.

TWO KINDS OF MAYONNAISE

Successful, delicious mayonnaise, without sugar, excess salt and preservatives, and with healthful oils, may be prepared several ways. The two mayonnaises that follow transform the plainest foods into highly pleasing, luscious-tasting delights. Just a little goes a long way.

REAL MAYONNAISE

1 egg yolk
5 ml/ 1 tsp Dijon mustard
2.5 ml/ ½ tsp fresh lemon juice
2.5 ml/ ½ tsp white or apple
 cider vinegar
1.25 ml/ ¼ tsp salt

Pinch of cayenne
125 ml/ 4 fl oz each Italian olive
 oil and peanut or corn oil
Black or white pepper, to taste

To prepare by hand: combine the first 6 ingredients plus 15 ml/ 1 Tbsp oil in a bowl. Whisk until well blended. While whisking, slowly dribble in the oil, a drop at a time, until half of oil is used. Then pour in a slow stream while whisking until thickened. Taste. Sprinkle with additional lemon juice and pepper to taste, and whisk again.

To prepare with food processor: fit the processor with a steel blade. Combine the first 6 ingredients and 15 ml/ 1 Tbsp oil. Process for 60 seconds. Pour 60 ml/ 2 fl oz oil into the top. Process until oil drips down. Dribble in remaining oil until thickened. Remove cover. Taste. Sprinkle with additional lemon juice and pepper to taste. Process for 5 seconds.

Each method prepares mayonnaise that is ready for immediate use. Store remaining mayonnaise in a tightly closed jar in refrigerator.

MAKES: about 250 g/ 8 oz

VARIATIONS: variations are endless; here are a few:

Aromatic Flavour Mayonnaise: substitute 1.25 ml/ ¼ tsp Spicy Mix (this chapter) for salt.

Tartare Sauce: stir into the finished mayonnaise 30 ml/ 2 Tbsp finely chopped shallot, 60 g/2 oz well-drained and chopped pickled gherkins, 15 ml/ 1 Tbsp finely chopped parsley and 10 ml/ 2 tsp well-rinsed chopped green olives.

Curry Mayonnaise: add 2.5 ml / ½ tsp mild curry powder and 15 ml/ 1 Tbsp finely chopped fresh tarragon, rosemary or basil (or 2.5 ml/ ½ tsp dried variety of any aforementioned herbs) after mixture is completely whipped. Wait 10 minutes before serving.

Aioli (Garlic Mayonnaise): stir into finished mayonnaise 5 ml/ 1 tsp finely chopped garlic. (Do not use dried garlic.)

Tomato/Chive Mayonnaise: stir into finished mayonnaise 30 ml/ 2 Tbsp finely chopped chives and 15 ml/ 1 Tbsp tomato purée.

LIGHT MAYONNAISE

150 ml/ 5 fl oz 'Canned'Chicken Stock (page 112), or stock made with low-sodium vegetable seasoning
7.5 ml/ 1 ½ tsp arrowroot
1 egg yolk
5 ml/ 1 tsp Dijon mustard
5 ml/ 1tsp fresh lemon juice
1.25 ml/ ¼ tsp salt

125ml/ 4 fl oz Italian olive and corn oil
5 ml/ 1tsp wine vinegar or apple cider vinegar
1.25 ml/ ½ tsp dried tarragon or oregano, crumbled
15 ml/ 1 Tbsp finely chopped fresh parsley or dill or a combination of both

1. Combine 30 ml/ 2 Tbsp cold stock with the arrowroot in a small bowl and stir to dissolve. Set aside. Heat the remaining stock in a heavy saucepan until simmering. Slowly whisk in the arrowroot mixture. Cook briefly until translucent and thickened. Remove from heat. Let cool.

2. To *finish by hand*: in a bowl, combine the egg yolk, mustard, lemon juice, salt and 15 ml/ 1 Tbsp oil. Whisk until well blended. Slowly dribble in the remaining oil a few drops at a time, until half the oil is used. Then pour in a slow, steady stream while whisking, until thickened. Sprinkle with the vinegar, tarragon or oregano and parsley. Whisk again. Whisk in the arrowroot mixture, a little at a time. The mayonnaise will be of the consistency on unchilled sour cream.

To *finish in food processor*: fit the processor with a steel blade. Combine the egg yolk, mustard, lemon juice, salt and 15 ml/ 1 Tbsp oil and process for 60 seconds. Add 60 ml/ 2 fl oz oil through the hole in the top and process until oil drips down. Add the remaining oil and process until all the oil is incorporated. Uncover, sprinkle with tarragon or oregano and parsley or dill. With the machine running, slowly pour the arrowroot mixture through feed tube.

Spoon the mayonnaise into a jar and refrigerate for several hours before using. The mixture will be fairly thick and will thicken further after chilling to spreadable consistency.

HEALTHY 'JUNK-FOOD' RECIPES

An asterisk (*) means that for a permanent place on the Basic All-Family Menu Plan (page 86), the recipe can be converted to an even more healthful one. See the instructions at the end of each recipe. The **letter K** means that the recipe is simple enough for your kids to make under your supervision.

CHEWY FRUIT MUESLI BARS

90 g/ 3 oz each dried
   unsweetened dates, dark
   raisins and dried apricots
   (without preservatives
   added), chopped
250 ml/ 8 fl oz unsweetened
   apple juice
2.5 ml/ ½ tsp each ground
   cinnamon and coriander
45 g/ 1 ½ oz rolled oats
30 g/ 1 oz unhulled sesame
   seeds

150 g/ 5 oz wholemeal flour
30 ml/ 2 Tbsp unprocessed bran
30 g/ 1 oz date powder
2.5 ml/ ½ tsp salt
125 g/ 4 oz almonds
1 egg
15 ml/ 1 Tbsp corn oil
15 ml/ 1 Tbsp honey (optional)
15 ml/1 Tbsp unsalted
   butter/margarine blend,
   melted

1. In heavy-based saucepan, bring the dates, raisins, apricots, apple juice and spices to boil. Reduce the heat to simmering. Cover and simmer for 5 minutes. Uncover and let cool. Pour into large mixing bowl.
2. Spread the oats and sesame seeds in a heated, well-seasoned cast-iron frying pan. Toast about 4 minutes until the seeds start to pop taking care not to let them burn. Turn into a bowl. Stir in the flour, date powder, salt and almonds. Let cool.
3. Beat together the egg, oil and optional honey to blend (use honey if you have a particularly sweet tooth). Stir into the bowl with cooled fruit mixture. Add the oatmeal mix, then beat for 1 minute or until combined (do not overbeat).
4. Pre-heat the oven to 350 °F/ 180 °C/Gas 4 and grease a 22.5 cm/ 9 inch square baking tin.
5. Spread the mixture in the pan, smoothing out the top with a moistened palette knife and pushing into the corners.
6. Bake for 30 minutes. Brush with the melted fat. Return to the oven and bake for 10 minutes. Place on a rack and let cool for 30 minutes. With a sharp knife, cut into 8 or 10 bars.

MAKES 8 or 10 bars

WONDER-FUL BREAD

500–530 g/ 16–17 oz strong
  plain flour
10 ml/ 2 tsp dried yeast
5 ml/ 1 tsp honey
180 ml/ 6 fl oz warm water
30 ml/ 2 Tbsp dried skimmed
  milk
1.25 ml/ ¼ tsp each salt and
  ground allspice
2.5 ml/ ½ tsp ground coriander
30 ml/ 2 Tbsp unsalted
  butter/margarine blend, cut
  into pieces

45 ml/ 3 Tbsp plain yoghurt
10 ml/ 2 tsp honey
30 ml/ 2 Tbsp frozen apple juice
  concentrate
1 egg white with 15 ml/ 1 Tbsp
  water
unhulled sesame seeds
  (optional)

1. In a tall glass, mix together the flour, yeast, honey and
   60 ml/ 2 fl oz warm water. Let stand 7 minutes until the
   mixture rises to the top of the glass.
2. Fit a food processor with a steel blade. Combine 500 g/ 1
   lb flour, dried milk, salt, spices and fat and process
   on/off 5 times.
3. Add the yeast mixture and process for 10 seconds. Add
   the yoghurt. Process for 10 seconds.
4. Add honey and apple juice concentrate to remaining 125
   ml/ 4 fl oz warm water and stir to dissolve, reheating, if
   necessary. With machine running, slowly pour through
   feed tube. Process until ball forms and rotates around
   bowl 15 times. (If dough doesn't congeal and remains
   sticky, remove cover of processor and sprinkle with
   remaining flour. Process on/off twice; then process for 15
   seconds.) Transfer dough to a lightly floured work
   surface and knead briefly. Shape into a ball.
5. Lightly oil a large bowl. Drop the dough ball in, turning
   to coat. Cover with cling film. Let rise at room
   temperature about 1 ¼ hours until double in bulk.
   Punch down and knead briefly on a lightly floured
   surface.
6. Cut into 3 equal parts. Shape each piece into a ball and
   flatten with your hands. Using a rolling pin, roll each
   piece into a rectangle wide enough to fit a loaf tin.
   Tightly roll up, pinching the ends. Lightly grease three
   500 g/ 1 lb loaf tins. Group the pans together and cover
   with a single sheet of lightly greased greaseproof paper.
7. Pre-heat the oven to 175 °F/ 190 °C/ Gas 5. Brush the
   dough with an egg wash; sprinkle with sesame seeds, if

desired. Bake for 25 to 30 minutes, or until lightly browned. Test for doneness. Remove from the tins and tap the bottoms of the loaves with knuckles. A hollow sound indicates loaves are done. If not, place the loaves directly on rack in oven and bake for 5 minutes. Let cool completely on rack before slicing.

MAKES: 3 mini-loaves

VARIATIONS: change the flour measurement to 450–500 g/ 15–16 oz. Add 75 g/ 2 ½ oz stoneground wholemeal flour. The finished bread will be more textured.

NOTES: dough may be cut in half in step 6, and shaped into 2 loaves, then baked for 30 to 35 minutes in 1 kg/ 2 lb loaf tin.

For a soft crust, reduce the baking time by 5 minutes, and wrap each fully cooled loaf in cling film. Let stand several hours before slicing.

SAUSAGES

350 g/ 12 oz boned pork tenderloin, partially trimmed
10 ml/ 2 tsp Spicy Mix (page 111)
1.25 ml/ ¼ tsp freshly grated nutmeg
2.5 ml/ ½ tsp salt
Pinch of freshly ground black pepper
15 ml/ 1 Tbsp finely chopped shallot
10 ml/ 2 tsp finely chopped garlic

3 whole cloves, crushed
30 ml/ 2 Tbsp fresh breadcrumbs or Shake and Bake-Alike (page 110)
5 ml/ 1 tsp each honey, tomato paste and apple cider vinegar
5 ml/ 1 tsp oil, plus 5 ml/ 1 tsp for sautéing
2.5 ml/ ½ tsp Dijon mustard
15 ml/ 1 Tbsp finely chopped fresh dill

1. Coarsely mince the meat with a mincer or food processor. If using food processor, cut meat into 3.5 cm/ 1 ½ inch cubes. Fit the food processor with a steel blade. Add the meat and process on/off until the meat is coarsely chopped. (Do not over-process to paste consistency.) Scrape into a bowl.
2. Combine the Spicy Mix and the nutmeg, salt, and black pepper. Sprinkle over the meat. Add the shallot, garlic and cloves and blend.
3. Combine and mash the breadcrumbs or Shake and Bake-Alike with the honey, tomato paste, vinegar, oil and mustard. Add to the meat and sprinkle with the dill.

Blend well with hands.

4. Divide the mixture into 14 equal portions. Shape into 10 cm/ 4 inch sausages by rolling between your palms. Arrange in one layer on a flat plate. Cover tightly and refrigerate for several hours or overnight to develop the flavour.

5. To cook, brush a non-stick frying pan with 5 ml/ 1 tsp oil and heat until hot. Over medium heat, lightly brown the sausages, uncovered, on all sides for 6 minutes. Reduce the heat. Cover and cook for 2 minutes. Drain on kitchen towels. Serve very hot.

MAKES: 14 sausages; serving size = 2 sausages

NOTES: shop-bought sausages contain sugar, large amounts of salt, pork fat and long list of additives, including indicted carcinogens, nitrates and nitrites. My delicious sausages are prepared without sugar or additives, and just a minimum of salt and pork fat. A word of caution: beware of chopped or minced pork that's packed with brine and then factory sealed. Use only freshly minced pork—preferably minced in your kitchen (your food processor does a fine job).

These sausages freeze well if tightly wrapped. Partially thaw them before cooking; use within 2 weeks.

* **TO CONVERT** into an even more healthful recipe, trim the pork to remove excess fat.

CUPPA-SOUP

30 ml/ 2 Tbsp Italian olive oil
180 g/ 6 oz Frozen Vegetable Mix (page 109)
750 ml/ 24 fl oz 'Canned' Chicken Stock (page 112) or stock made with low-sodium vegetable seasoning
375 g/12 oz canned tomatoes, crushed
75 g/ 1 ½ oz potatoes, finely diced
5 ml/ 1 tsp balsamic vinegar

1 pinch each of salt and pepper
1.25 ml/ ¼ tsp ground coriander
5 ml/1 tsp dried basil, crushed
75 g/ 2 ½ oz shelled fresh peas
60 g/ 2 oz thin spaghetti, broken up
60 g/ 2 oz courgette, unpeeled and finely chopped
Freshly grated Parmesan cheese

1. Heat the oil in a large heavy-bottomed saucepan until hot but not smoking. Add the Vegetable Mix and sauté until soft over medium-high heat about 4 minutes.
2. Add the chicken stock, tomatoes, potatoes, vinegar, salt, pepper and herbs. Bring to the simmering point, cover and simmer for 10 minutes.
3. Add the peas, spaghetti and courgette. Bring to the simmering point again. Stir well. Cover and simmer for 20 minutes, stirring from time to time. Remove from heat and let stand, covered, for 10 minutes. Reheat, if necessary, before serving.
4. Ladle the soup into plates, and sprinkle with Parmesan cheese.

MAKES: 1.3 to 1.5 litres/ 46 to 50 fl oz; serves 5 to 6

POPCORN (K)

150 g/ 5 oz popping corn
5 ml/ 1 tsp oil
45 ml/ 3 Tbsp unsalted
   butter/margarine blend

15 ml/ 1 Tbsp Seasoning Mix
   (page 110)
15–30 ml/ 1–2 Tbsp freshly
   grated Parmesan cheese

1. Pop the corn in popcorn maker, or pop as follows: spread oil into well-seasoned cast-iron frying pan. Heat over medium-high heat for 3 minutes. Sprinkle with the corn, spreading it out into one layer. Cover and pop, shaking the pan around several times until the popping ceases. Turn into a large bowl.
2. Over low heat, in small heavy-based saucepan, melt the fat. Stir in the Seasoning Mix and cook until bubbly. Remove from the heat and let stand for 1 minute.
3. Slowly pour the seasoned butter/margarine blend over the popcorn until well coated, stirring. Sprinkle with cheese to taste and stir again. Serve warm.

MAKES: about 4 large servings

SERVING SUGGESTIONS: use as croûtons with soup, and as accompaniments to salads and sandwiches. Take along a batch to the cinema.

* MUSHROOM PIZZA

Dough:

335–350 g/ 11–12 oz strong
   plain flour plus extra flour for
   work surface
75 g/ 2 ½ oz wholemeal flour
1.25 ml/ ¼ tsp salt
10 ml/ 2 tsp dried skimmed milk
15 ml/ 1 Tbsp freshly grated
   Parmesan cheese
250 ml/ 8 fl oz warm water
10 ml/ 2 tsp dried yeast
30 ml/ 2 Tbsp Italian olive oil
   plus extra oil for bowl and
   brushing over dough

Topping:

30 ml/ 2 Tbsp Italian olive oil
1 medium onion, quartered and
   thinly sliced
10 ml/ 2 tsp finely chopped
   garlic
1 green or red pepper, seeded,
   cored, quartered and thinly
   sliced
2.5 ml/ ½ tsp each dried sweet
   basil and oregano leaves
125 g/ 4 oz button mushrooms,
   ends trimmed, rinsed, dried
   and thinly sliced
350 g/ 12 oz mozzarella cheese
600 ml/ 20 fl oz Parmesan
   cheese, freshly grated
20g/ ⅔ oz finely chopped
   fresh parsley

Sauce:

About 600 ml/ 20 fl oz warm
   Pizza Sauce or Spaghetti
   Sauce (page 125)

1. To prepare the dough, use a food processor fitted with a steel blade. Add the 335 g/ 11 oz plain flour, all of the wholemeal flour, salt, dried milk and Parmesan cheese and process on/off 3 times.
2. Pour warm water into a small bowl. Sprinkle with the yeast, stirring until dissolved. Add 30 ml/ 2 Tbsp oil and stir quickly. With machine running, pour mixture through feed tube and process for 15 seconds. Sprinkle with 46 g/ 1 ½ oz flour and process for 10 seconds. The dough will partially clean the sides of the bowl and will be sticky.
3. Scrape the dough on to a work surface sprinkled with 30 ml/ 2 Tbsp flour. Knead for about 2 minutes (see Notes), adding another 30 ml/ 2 Tbsp flour, if necessary, to make a soft, smooth, elastic dough. (Just the right amount of flour and proper kneading will make a crispy crust.) Shape into a ball.
4. Lightly oil a large bowl. Drop the ball into the bowl, turning to coat. Cover with cling film. Let rise at room temperature 1 ¾ to 2 hours until puffy and light. Knock

back. Cut into 2 pieces. Shape into balls, cover with greaseproof paper and refrigerate.

5. Prepare the topping by heating the oil in well-seasoned cast-iron frying pan until hot. Add the onion, garlic, pepper and herbs. Stir and sauté without browning. Combine the mushrooms with mixture and sauté until all liquid has evaporated.

6. Pre-heat the oven to 230°C/450°F/Gas 8 and lightly grease two 25 cm/10 inch pizza pans. Lightly flour a work surface. Roll each ball of dough into .5 cm/ ¼ inch thick rounds. Put the dough into the pans and brush with oil. Bake for 5 minutes, then remove from oven leaving oven on.

7. To assemble, spread each just-prepared pizza with 180 ml/ 6 fl oz warm sauce. Top with mozzarella cheese, then dribble with the remaining sauce. Sprinkle with Parmesan cheese, parsley, and then topping. Bake on lowest rack in the already-hot oven for 15 to 20 minutes, or until cheese is bubbly and shell is crisp. Cut into wedges with pizza cutter or sharp shears, and serve immediately.

MAKES: 2 pizzas; 4 to 6 wedges per pizza

VARIATIONS: variations are endless. Here are a few: add sautéed tiny meatballs, sautéed chicken pieces, rare cooked beef or pork pieces, cubed tofu, lightly sautéed prawns, broken up and lightly sautéed Sausages (page 119) to the topping in step 5.

NOTES: if low-sodium tomato products are used, add 1.25 ml/ ¼ tsp salt in step 5, if desired.

Here's how to knead: push the dough down and forwards with the heel of your hand; then fold the dough over towards you. Make a quarter turn, and push and fold as before. Repeat turning, pushing and folding until the texture of the dough becomes smooth and elastic, and can be easily shaped into a non-sticky ball.

* **TO CONVERT** into an even more healthy recipe, lower the fat content by reducing the mozzarella cheese to 180 g/ 6 oz. Keep the flavour high by increasing dried basil and oregano to 3.75 ml/ ¾ tsp each, and adding a pinch of salt to topping if desired. Also used converted versions of Pizza Sauce or Spaghetti Sauce (look for the asterisk at the end of the recipes).

* PIZZA SAUCE (K)

30 ml/ 2 Tbsp Italian olive oil
180 g/ 16 oz Frozen
  vegetable Mix (page 109)
125 g/ 4 oz snow-white fresh
  mushrooms, ends trimmed,
  rinsed, dried and coarsely
  chopped
600 g/ 1¼ lb can Italian
  tomatoes with basil

1.25 ml/ ¼ tsp salt
1 bay leaf, wrapped in muslin
  and tied
45 ml/ 3 Tbsp tomato paste,
  preferably without added salt
10 ml/ 2 tsp dried oregano,
  crushed

1. In a large heavy-based saucepan, heat the oil over
   moderately high heat until hot but not smoking. Add the
   Vegetable Mix and cook and stir until most of liquid
   evaporates. Add the mushrooms and cook for 3 minutes,
   stirring often.
2. Stir in the tomatoes, breaking up with large spoon. Add
   the remaining ingredients and combine. Bring to the
   boil, reduce the heat to simmering and simmer,
   uncovered, for 30 minutes, stirring from time to time.
   Remove from the heat and stir. Cover and let stand for
   10 minutes. Discard the bay leaf bundle.

MAKES: about 1 litre/ 32 fl oz, serving size = 180 ml/6 fl oz

VARIATION: add 5 ml/1 tsp tarragon vinegar and 2.5 ml/ ½
tsp curry powder in step 2. Wonderful new flavour!

NOTE: if tomatoes prepared with basil are not available,
substitute 15 ml/ 1 Tbsp finely chopped fresh basil, or 7.5
ml/ 1 ½ tsp dried basil to the unseasoned canned tomatoes.
Fresh basil, though is preferable.

* **TO CONVERT** into an even more healthful recipe, reduce
the salt content by using canned Italian tomatoes with
basil, no salt added, and adding only a pinch of salt.

* SPAGHETTI SAUCE

1 small carrot, peeled and
  trimmed
2 medium onions
1 small green or red pepper,
  seeded
2 large garlic cloves
45 ml/ 3 Tbsp Italian olive oil
500g/1 lb lean beef, minced
7.5 ml/1 ½ tsp each dried
  oregano and basil, crushed
1.25 ml/ ¼ tsp salt
Pinch of cayenne pepper
  (optional)

10 ml/ 2 tsp wine vinegar or
  balsamic vinegar
1 kg/ 2 lb canned Italian
  tomatoes
180 g/ 16 oz canned tomato
  paste, preferably without salt
  added
350 ml/ 12 fl oz 'Canned'
  Chicken Stock (page 112) or
  stock made with low-sodium
  vegetable seasoning

1. Use a food processor to chop the vegetables. Cut the carrot, onions and green or red pepper into uniform pieces. Halve the garlic cloves. Fit the food processor with a steel blade. Place the cut ingredients in the container and process on/off about 4 times, or until mixture is finely chopped (take care not to purée).
2. Heat the oil in well-seasoned cast-iron frying pan until hot. Sauté the vegetable mixture until softened but not brown, stirring constantly.
3. Add the meat, breaking up pieces with large spoon. Sprinkle with herbs and spices. Stir and sauté until lightly browned and all liquid has evaporated. Pour the vinegar around the sides of the frying pan. Cook for 1 minute.
4. Partly purée the tomato solids (reserving the liquid), and tomato paste in the food processor. Pour into the frying pan. Add the reserved liquid from can and the Chicken Stock. Bring to the boil. Reduce the heat to simmering, partially cover and simmer fos 1 ¼ hours, stirring from time to time.

MAKES: about 1.5 litres/ 50 fl oz;
serving size = 180 ml/ 6 fl oz

VARIATION: if you have Sausages (page 119) to hand, use 4 of them, and reduce the minced meat weight to 350 g/ 12 oz.

* TO CONVERT into an even more healthy recipe, reduce the salt content by using canned Italian tomatoes, no salt added, and adding only a pinch of salt.

*BEEFBURGERS (K)

120 g/ 10 oz lean minced beef
45 g/ 1 ½ oz Shake and
  Bake-Alike (page 110)
60 ml/ 2 fl oz tomato purée,
  preferably low-sodium
45 ml/3 Tbsp finely chopped
  shallot or onion
5 ml/ 1 tsp finely chopped garlic
1.25 ml/ ¼ tsp salt

2.5 ml/ ½ tsp Spicy Mix (page
111)
15 ml/ 1 Tbsp oil
4 bought hamburger buns or
  Hamburger Buns (page 136)
Real Mayonnaise (page 114)
Thinly sliced cucumber
Thinly sliced tomatoes
Thinly sliced onions

1. Combine and blend the beef with the Shake and
   Bake-Alike , tomato purée, shallots or onions, garlic and
   salt. Divide into 4 equal portions. Shape into patties.
   Sprinkle each patty on both sides with equal amounts of
   Spicy Mix, pressing into meat.
   If you're using a frying pan: rub the oil across a non-stick
   frying pan. Heat until hot but not smoking. Sauté the
   meat, turning every 2 minutes. Cook to desired
   doneness (7 to 8 minutes for medium rare.)
   If you're using a grill or barbecue: brush the meat lightly
   with oil. Grill on each side for 4 minutes or place on a
   barbecue grid and cook over the coals, turning every 2
   minutes. Cook to desired doneness.
2. Split the buns and lightly toast. Spread with
   mayonnaise. Serve burgers on buns between layers of
   cucumber, tomatoes and onions.

SERVES 4

VARIATION: Beefburgers with Cheese Stuffing: divide meat
into 8 equal portions in step 1. Shape into 1 cm/ ½ inch
patties. In a bowl, combine and blend 60 g/ 2 oz grated
mature Cheddar cheese with 2.5 ml/ ½ tsp each
Worcestershire sauce and Dijon mustard. Spread equal
amounts of stuffing over the 4 patties. Cover the remaining
4 patties, pinching the edges all around to seal. Continue
with recipe.

* TO CONVERT into an even more healthful recipe, lower
the fat content by replacing Real Mayonnaise with Light
Mayonnaise (page 115).

FISH AND PRAWN FINGERS

1 egg
15 ml/ 1 Tbsp each fresh lemon
    juice and water
5 ml/ 1tsp corn or peanut oil
    1.25 ml/ ¼ tsp each salt and
    onion powder
45 ml/ 3 Tbsp cornflour
60 g/ 2 oz breadcrumbs,
    preferably homemade (page
    133), or Shake and
    Bake-Alike (page 110)

250 g/ 8 oz medium prawns,
    peeled, deveined and well
    drained
250 g/ 8 oz thick cod or halibut
    fillet, cut into 1 cm/ ½ inch
    strips
60 ml/ 4 Tbsp peanut oil
Finely chopped fresh parsley
½ lemon, plus lemon wedges
    for garnish

1. Place the egg, lemon juice, water, 5 ml/ 1 tsp peanut oil, salt, and onion powder in shallow dish and beat with fork to blend. Set aside.
2. Cut 2 large pieces of greaseproof paper. On one piece, spread the cornflour; on another sheet, spread out the breadcrumbs or Shake and Bake-Alike.
3. Coat the prawn and fish fingers individually in cornflour, shaking off excess. Then dip them in egg mixture, coating well. Dredge each piece in crumbs or Shake and Bake-Alike, pressing to hold the crumbs. Chill in freezer for 10 minutes.
4. Use 2 non-stick frying pans so the prawns and fish fingers may be cooked in one layer without crowding. Heat 15 ml/ 1 Tbsp oil in a non-stick frying pan. Start to cook the fish fingers, as they require more cooking time, arranging the fish in one layer. Cook on one side about 4 minutes until lightly browned. Add another 15 ml/ 1 Tbsp oil and turn.
5. Start cooking the prawns in a second frying pan after turning the fish fingers. Heat 15 ml/1 Tbsp oil in non-stick frying pan arranging the prawns in one layer. Cook 2 ½ to 3 minutes until browned. Turn, then add the remaining oil. Cook until delicately browned (do not overcook or the prawns will become tough).
6. Arrange the fish and prawns on a platter. Sprinkle with the parsley and lemon juice and garnish with lemon wedges.

SERVES 4

* CREAMY MASHED POTATOES (K)

500 ml/ 1 lb baking potatoes, peeled and cut into 2.5 cm/ 1 inch cubes	Pinch of salt
	30 ml/ 2 Tbsp light cream
	60 g/ 2 oz plain yoghurt
20 ml/ 4 tsp unsalted butter/margarine blend	Onion or spring onions, finely chopped
1.25 ml/ ¼ tsp each dried dill and mild paprika	60 ml/4 Tbsp finely grated Cheddar cheese

1. In a large heavy-based saucepan, cook the potatoes in rapidly boiling water 8 to 10 minutes until firm-tender. Drain well. Wipe out the saucepan and return the potatoes to the pan. Cook over medium-high heat, shaking the potatoes around the pan for about 15 seconds to dry any excess moisture. Remove from the heat.
2. Add 10 ml/ 2 tsp butter/margarine blend, dill, paprika and salt, Mash until smooth. Add the cream and mash again. Stir in the yoghurt , onion or spring onion and 45 ml/3 Tbsp cheese. Let cool.
3. Pile into side dishes, mounding on top. Sprinkle with the remaining grated cheese and dot with the remaining butter/margarine blend.

SERVES 4

* TO CONVERT into an even more healthful recipe, reduce the fat content by substituting milk for cream, and reducing the Cheddar cheese by half, reserving 15 ml/ 1 Tbsp for topping (step 3).

CHIPS (K)

3 medium baking potatoes, about 500 g/ 1 lb peeled and cut into 1cm/ ½ inch strips	7.5 ml/ 1 ½ tsp finely chopped garlic (optional)
30 ml/ 2 Tbsp olive oil or corn oil	5 ml/ 1 tsp Spicy Mix (page 111)
45 ml/ 3 Tbsp finely chopped shallots	6.25 ml/ 1 ¼ tsp balsamic or red wine vinegar

1. Pre-heat the oven to 230°C/450°F/Gas 8. Lay the cut potatoes on kitchen towels and dry well.
2. Brush the oil over a baking tray. Place the pan in oven for 5 minutes, then add the potatoes in one layer. Sprinkle with the shallots, garlic and Spicy Mix, turning with a palette knife several times to evenly coat. Bake for 5 minutes, then turn. Bake for another 5 minutes.
3. Sprinkle with the vinegar, turning several times. Turn the oven heat up to 240°C/475°F/Gas 9 and bake the potatoes for 8 to 10 minutes more, or until lightly browned and tender. Serve immediately.

SERVES 4

VARIATION: in step 3, omit the vinegar, sprinkle potatoes with 15 ml/ 1 Tbsp freshly grated Parmesan cheese.

KETCHUP DE-LITE (K)

250 ml/ 8 oz tomato purée
30 ml/ 2 Tbsp tomato paste
15 ml/ 1 Tbsp Italian olive oil or
corn oil
2.5 ml/ ½ tsp ground ginger
7.5 ml/ 1 ½ tsp apple cider vinegar
10 ml/ 2 tsp honey
15 ml/ 1 Tbsp finely chopped fresh parsley
Pinch of cayenne pepper
1.25 ml/ ¼ tsp salt (optional)

1. Place the tomato purée and tomato paste in a bowl. Beat with a whisk to blend. Add the remaining ingredients, one at a time, whisking after each addition. Cover and let stand for 30 minutes before using.
2. Refrigerate in a tightly closed jar. This ketchup will keep in the refrigerator for up to 2 weeks.

MAKES: 300 g/ 10 oz; serving size = 60 ml/ 4 Tbsp

VARIATIONS: add 2.5 ml/ ½ tsp chilli powder or chilli con carne seasoning and 30 ml/ 2 Tbsp chopped shallot or onion.

Russian Dressing: combine equal amounts of Ketchup De-Lite with Real Mayonnaise (page 114).

SALAD DRESSING (K)

75 ml/ 2 ½ fl oz balsamic
vinegar or red wine vinegar
75 ml/2 ½ fl oz tomato juice,
preferably low-sodium (see
Note)
75 ml/ 2 ½ fl oz Italian olive oil
7.5 ml/ 1 ½ tsp Spicy Mix
(page 111) or Seasoning Mix
(page 110)

30 ml/ 2 Tbsp fresh lemon juice
15 ml/ 1 Tbsp finely chopped
shallot
1.25 ml/ ¼ tsp salt (optional)

1. Combine all the ingredients in a jar and shake well.
2. Let stand at room temperature for 30 minutes before
serving. Store in refrigerator.

MAKES: a little more than 250 ml/ 8 fl oz; serving size = 30
ml/ 2 Tbsp

NOTE: I choose the low-sodium variety of tomato juice
because of its pure natural tomato flavour. If you prefer the
regular variety with added salt, omit the 1.25 ml/ ¼ tsp
salt.

* CRISPY FISH FILLETS

600 g/ 1 ¼ lb thin plaice fillets,
   each cut in half (see Note)
30 ml/ 2 Tbsp fresh lemon juice
10 ml/ 2 Tbsp frozen orange
   juice concentrate
60 ml/ 2 fl oz evaporated milk
Pinch of salt

150 g/ 5 oz Shake and
   Bake-Alike (page 110)
30 ml/ 2 Tbsp peanut or corn oil
Lemon wedges
Real Mayonnaise (page 114)
   (optional)

1. Wash the fish thoroughly and dry with kitchen towels. Place in a rectangular baking dish and spread out into one layer. Sprinkle with lemon juice, turning to coat. Then set aside to marinate for 15 minutes.
2. In a shallow bowl, combine the orange juice concentrate, milk and salt. Beat with a fork to blend.
3. Sprinkle half the Shake and Bake-Alike over a piece of greaseproof paper. Dip each fillet into the orange mixture, they lay on top of the Shake and Bake-Alike, pressing to adhere. Sprinkle the fish with remaining mix and press to adhere. Cover with another sheet of greaseproof paper. Lay the package on a plate and place in the freezing compartment for 10 to 15 minutes to set.
4. Using a large frying pan, heat 15 ml/ 1 Tbsp oil until hot. Add the fish in one layer and sauté about 3 minutes until lightly browned. Turn. Add the remaining 15 ml/ 1 Tbsp oil and sauté for 3 minutes.
5. To make a regular 'TV dinner' serve Crispy Fish Fillets with Creamy Mashed Potatoes or Chips (pages 128 and 129) and Frozen Vegetable Mix (page 109), or a vegetable of choice. When ready to serve, garnish with lemon wedges. Serve with Real Mayonnaise (page 114) on the side, if desired.

SERVES 4

NOTES: any firm-fleshed thinly sliced fish, such as sea bass or halibut, may be substituted for the plaice.

If the fillets don't fit your frying pan in one layer without crowding, cook in 2 batches, using a total of 15 ml/1 Tbsp oil for each batch.

* TO CONVERT into a more healthful recipe, reduce the fat content by substituting Light Mayonnaise (page 115) for Real Mayonnaise.

* 'CANNED' TOMATO SOUP

30 ml/ 2 Tbsp oil
30 ml/ 2 Tbsp finely chopped
   shallot
500 ml/ 16 fl oz 'Canned'
   Chicken Stock (page 112) or
   stock made with low-sodium
   vegetable seasoning
500 ml/ 16 oz canned tomatoes
30 ml/ 2 Tbsp unsweetened
   apple juice
1.25 ml/ ¼ oz each freshly
   grated nutmeg, dried
   tarragon, crushed, and salt

1 bay leaf
125 ml/ 4 fl oz single cream or
   equal amounts of cream and
   milk
30 ml/ 2 Tbsp arrowroot
   dissolved in 30 ml/ 2 Tbsp
   water (see NOTE)
75 g/ 2 ½ oz cooked brown rice
10 ml/ 2 tsp honey (optional)
Freshly ground black pepper to
   taste
15 ml/ 1 Tbsp finely chopped
   parsley or dill

1. In a large heavy-based saucepan, heat the oil until hot.
   Add the shallot and sauté over medium heat until
   softened but not brown, stirring continually.
2. Add the stock, tomatoes, apple juice, nutmeg, tarragon,
   salt and bay leaf. Bring to the boil, then reduce the heat
   to simmering; cover and simmer for 15 minutes.
3. Pour the soup into a food mill with bowl underneath
   and purée. Return the purée to the saucepan over low
   heat. Whisk in the cream then bring to the simmering
   point. While whisking, dribble in half the arrowroot
   mixture, and cook until the soup begins to thicken. Add
   the remaining arrowroot if you prefer a thicker
   consistency.

* COPY CAT CHICKEN McNUGGETS

1 egg
30 ml/ 2 Tbsp unsweetened
   apple juice
30 ml/ 2 Tbsp single cream
1.25 ml/ ¼ tsp salt
20 g/ ¾ oz fine breadcrumbs,
   preferably homemade (see
   NOTE)
30 ml/ 2 Tbsp flour

3.75 ml/ ¾ tsp each dried
   rosemary, crushed, and
   onion powder
1.25 ml/ ¼ tsp each ground
   ginger and curry powder
600 g/ 1 ¼ lb thick chicken
   breasts, boned and skinned
4 large garlic cloves
½ lemon

1. Combine and blend the egg, apple juice and cream. In another bowl, place the salt, breadcrumbs, flour, rosemary and spices, stirring to combine. Spread the mixture across a freezerproof flat plate.
2. Wash and dry the chicken thoroughly. Cut into 2.5 cm/ 1 inch chunks. Drop into the egg mixture, drain each piece and then dip into the crumb mixture, rolling to evenly coat. Place the plate in the freezing compartment uncovered, for 10 minutes to set.
3. Sauté in 2 batches. Heat 15 ml/ 1 Tbsp oil in a large well-seasoned cast-iron frying pan until hot but not smoking. Add half the garlic and cook for 1 minute, stirring continually. Remove and discard garlic with slotted spoon. Add half the chicken and cook until lightly browned on both sides, rolling when necessary to brown all areas (total cooking time 6 minutes). Transfer to a warm oven or to a plate over simmering water while the second batch is cooking (do not cover).
4. To prepare the second batch, add the remaining oil to the pan (it will heat rapidly). Sauté the remaining garlic and continue to cook as in step 3. Squeeze lemon juice over the chicken and serve immediately.

SERVES 4

NOTE: make your own breadcrumbs. It's easy. Use 3 to 4 slices French bread, or 3 thick slices Wonder-Ful Bread (page 118). Cut into 1 cm/ ½ inch cubes. Spread on baking sheet and bake in a pre-heated 425°F/220°C/Gas 7 oven for 8 to 10 minutes, turning once with a palette knife. Let cool and transfer to a blender and blend on high speed for 1 minute. Use immediately, or pour into jar, tightly close and store in refrigerator (up to 2 weeks).

* TO CONVERT into an even more healthful recipe, reduce the fat by substituting equal amount milk for cream.

* 'FRIED' CHICKEN

15 ml/ 1 Tbsp fresh lemon
juice
30 ml/ 2 Tbsp frozen orange
juice concentrate
30 ml/ 2 Tbsp evaporated milk
15 ml/ 1 Tbsp water
1.5 kg/ 3 lb chicken, skinned,
wings removed and cut into
eight pieces

75 ml/ 2 ½ oz Shake and
Bake-alike (page 110)
30 ml/2 Tbsp unsalted
15 ml/ 1 Tbsp unsalted
butter/margarine blend, cut
into small pieces
45 g/ 1 ½ oz mature Cheddar
cheese, finely grated

1. Combine the first 4 ingredients and blend with a fork.
2. Pierce the chicken all over with a fork. Add to the bowl, turning to coat well. Cover and let stand for 1 hour at room temperature. Drain each piece of chicken, then lay on a double sheet of kitchen paper and gently blot (do not rub), so the chicken is still moist.
3. Sprinkle half the Shake and Bake-Alike over a large plate. Lay the chicken pieces on top of the mixture, pressing to adhere. Sprinkle with the remaining mix, pressing into chicken all over. Refrigerate, uncovered, for 30 minutes or longer.
4. Pre-heat the oven to 220°C/425°F/Gas 7. Spread the oil over a shallow baking tin large enough to hold chicken in one layer. Place the tin in the oven for 7 minutes. Reduce the heat to 200°C/400°F/Gas6. Immediately arrange the chicken in one layer and dot with the fat. Bake for 20 minutes. Carefully turn with a fish slice, scooping up so that the browned pieces remain on chicken. Return to the oven and bake for 10 minutes more. Sprinkle with the cheese and bake for another 10 to 15 minutes, or until browned and cooked through.

SERVES 4 to 5

VARIATION: add 5 ml/ 1 tsp dried sage to Shake and Bake-Alike (step 3)

NOTE: chicken is delicious served cold. If you're planning to serve it cold, add 1.25 ml/ ¼ tsp salt to Shake and Bake-Alike before coating the chicken.

* TO CONVERT into an even more healthful recipe, reduce the fat content by substituting 30 ml/ 2 Tbsp freshly grated Parmesan cheese, for the Cheddar cheese.

* LASAGNE (K)

250 ml/ 8 oz lasagne noodles
7.5 ml/ 1 ½ tsp oil
1.25 ml/ ¼ tsp salt
Unsalted butter/margarine
   blend
1 litre/ 32 fl oz Spaghetti Sauce
(page 125)
250 g/ 8 oz mozzarella
   cheese, thinly sliced

450 g/ 15 oz ricotta cheese, at
   room temperature
60 g/ 2 oz Parmesan cheese,
   freshly grated
30 g/ 1 oz Cheddar cheese,
   finely grated
15 g/ ½ oz finely chopped fresh
   basil (see Note)

1. To cook the noodles, bring large saucepan of water to boil. Add 5 ml/ 1 tsp oil and salt. Carefully ease 2 to 3 noodles at a time into water and boil 8 to 10 minutes, until just cooked. Pour into a colander and drain. Rinse under cold running water and drain again.
2. Grease a 17.5 x 22.5 cm / 7 x 9 inch ovenproof dish with the butter/margarine blend. Spoon a thin layer of Spaghetti Sauce over the base and arrange one-third of the noodles in one layer over the sauce. Spread one-third of the sauce over the noodles. Lay one-third of the mozzarella cheese over the sauce. Cover with one-third of the ricotta cheese, spreading out with a knife. Sprinkle with one-third of each Parmesan, Cheddar cheese and basil. Repeat the layering sequence twice more.
3. Pre-heat the oven 190°C/375°F/Gas 5. Cover the dish with aluminium foil and bake for 20 minutes. Reduce the heat to 180°C/350°F/Gas 4. Uncover and bake for 20 to 50 minutes, or until bubbly and hot. Cut and serve at once.

SERVES 8 to 10

VARIATION: for a meatless lasagne, substitute Pizza Sauce (page 124) for the Spaghetti Sauce.

NOTE: fresh herbs enhance flavour. If fresh basil isn't available, substitute finely chopped fresh rosemary, dill or parsley.

HAMBURGER BUNS

450 g/ 15 oz strong plain flour
5 mm/ 3 tsp plus 15 ml/ 1 Tbsp
  honey
10 ml/ 2 tsp dried yeast
180 ml–250 ml/ 6–8 fl oz warm
  water
75 g/ 2 ½ oz stoneground
  wholemeal flour
2.5 ml/ ½ tsp salt

1.25 ml/ ¼ tsp ground cinnamon
15 ml/ 1 Tbsp dried skimmed
  milk
75 ml/ 2 ½ fl oz corn or peanut
  oil
2 eggs
Unhulled sesame seeds
  (optional)

1. In a tall glass, combine and blend 30 ml/ 2 Tbsp flour, 5
   ml/ 1 tsp honey, yeast and 60 ml/ 2 fl oz warm water.
   Let stand about 7 minutes until mixture rises to top of
   glass.
2. Fit a food processor with a steel blade. combine 400 g/ 14
   oz flour, all the wholemeal flour, salt, cinnamon, dried
   milk and 10 ml/ 2 tsp honey. Sprinkle with the oil and
   process on/off 4 times.
3. Add the yeast and process about 10 seconds until
   blended.
4. Combine 15 ml/ 1 Tbsp honey and 1 egg. With the
   machine running, pour the mixture through the feed
   tube. Process for 3 seconds, then start the processor
   again and dribble in enough remaining warm water to
   make a soft, smooth non-sticky ball. Process until the
   ball rotates around the bowl 10 to 14 times. If the dough
   is still sticky, sprinkle the work surface with remaining
   flour. Transfer the dough to the work surface and knead
   briefly until the dough is no longer sticky. Shape into a
   ball.
5. Lightly oil a large bowl, and drop the dough in. Turn to
   coat. Cover with cling film and let rise at room
   temperature about 1 hour until double in bulk. Knock
   back, then knead briefly, squeezing out the bubbles. Cut
   in half, then cut each half into 6 equal portions. Cover
   with cling film and let rest for 5 minutes.
6. Lightly grease 2 baking trays and 2 pieces of greaseproof
   paper. Shape each dough piece into a smooth ball and
   place on the paper. With the palm of hand flatten the
   balls to 8.5 cm/ 3 ½ inch diameter. Cover with
   greaseproof paper and let stand about 50 minutes until
   doubled.
7. Pre-heat the oven to 375°F/ 190°C/Gas 5. Beat the
   remaining egg with 15 ml/ 1 Tbsp water. Using a pastry

brush, brush each bun with the egg wash. Sprinkle with sesame seeds, if desired. Bake for 12 to 15 minutes, or until lightly browned. (If you like your buns crunchy, bake for 20 minutes.) Cool on a rack.

MAKES: 12 buns

SERVING SUGGESTION: split and use as a sandwich bread. Toast, if desired.

VARIATION: the dough makes excellent loaves, too. For 2 loaves, cut dough in half at the end of step 5. Shape each half into ball. Flatten with hands. Using a rolling pin, roll each piece into a rectangle wide enough to fit into a loaf tin. Tightly roll up, pinching the ends. Place join down in 2 lightly greased 1 kg/ 2 lb loaf tins. Cover with greased greaseproof paper and let rise until well above side of tin. Brush with an egg wash, and sprinkle with sesame seeds, if desired. Bake for about 35 minutes in a pre-heated oven. Test for doneness: remove from tins and tap bottom of loaves with knuckles. A hollow sound indicates loaves are done. Let loaves cool completely before slicing.

DESSERT TOPPING

180 ml/ 6 fl oz plain yoghurt
45 ml/ 3 Tbsp single cream
1.25 ml/ ¼ tsp ground cin-
    namon
Pinch of freshly grated nutmeg

15 ml/ 1 Tbsp unsweetened
    desiccated coconut
7.5 ml/ 1 ½ tsp honey

Combine all the ingredients in a small bowl. Gently fold in the ingredients (do not beat) and let stand for 10 minutes before serving. Serve chilled.

MAKES 250 ml/ 8 fl oz; serving size = up to 60 ml/ 2 fl oz

SERVING SUGGESTION: great with breakfast pancakes or over fresh or dried fruit.

* HAPPY BIRTHDAY CAKE

Imagine—a rich, sweet-tasting, creamy-iced birthday cake that uses less than 5 ml/ 1 tsp sugar per serving. Most shop-bought and homemade cakes use at least 16 times that much per serving.

The icing is a clone of dark, chocolate fudge buttercream, but it has none of the health-drawbacks of its conventional counterpart. Chocolate is replaced by carob, a naturally sweet plant which tastes like chocolate in this confection; and the butter content is reduced. Use the icing also for a low-sugar healthful chocolate-brown smooth fudge sauce over ice cream, custard, fruit or plain cake.

Serve this cake unadorned by icing any day for a scrumptious treat.

Cake:
125 g/ 4 oz unsalted
   butter/margarine blend, plus
   enough to grease tins
30 ml/ 2 Tbsp corn oil
125 g/ 4 oz Fruit Butter
   (page 112)
250 g/ 8 oz mashed ripe
   bananas (2 medium
   bananas)
10 ml/ 2 Tbsp pure vanilla
   essence
4 eggs, separated
540 g/ 18 oz Batter and Cake
   Mix (page 108)
5ml/ 1 tsp bicarbonate of soda
5 ml/ 1 tsp ground ginger
350 ml/ 12 fl oz milk
30 g/ 1 oz walnuts, finely
   chopped
30 g/ 1 oz carob powder
5 ml/ 1 tsp ground cinnamon
Pinch of cream of tartar

Fudge Icing:
75 g/ 6 oz unsweetened carob
   chips (available in
   health-food shops)
3.75 ml/ ⅗ tsp ground cinnamon
1.25 ml/ ¼ tsp salt
90 ml/ 6 Tbsp honey
22.5 ml/ 4 ½ tsp sugar
5 cm/2 inch length vanilla pod,
   split
15 ml/ 3 Tbsp instant coffee
3 egg yolks
180 ml/ 6 fl oz evaporated milk
250 g/ 8 fl oz plus 30 ml/ 2
   Tbsp butter/margarine blend
Decoration:
Desiccated unsweetened
coconut
Blanched almond halves or
   plastic Happy Birthday
   decoration

1. Place the first 5 ingredients in a large bowl and beat with an electric mixer on medium speed to 1 minute, then on high speed until light and fluffy, scraping down the sides of the bowl when necessary.
2. Reduce the speed to medium. Add the egg yolks and beat for 1 minute, scrape down the sides of the bowl.

3. Combine the Batter and Cake Mix with the bicarbonate of soda and ginger. Add to the batter alternately with the milk, 25 ml/ 4 fl oz at a time. Stop the machine and scrape down the sides.
4. Combine the walnuts, date powder and cinnamon. Sprinkle over the batter with a wooden spoon, stir using 5 to 6 broad strokes.
5. Beat the egg white until foamy. Sprinkle in the cream of tartar and continue beating until stiff but not dry peaks form. Fold one-third into the batter then fold in the balance, using as few strokes as possible.
6. Pre-heat the oven to 180°C/350°F/Gas 4. Pour the batter into two round loose bottomed 20 cm/ 8 inch layer tins. Bake for 45 minutes, or until a toothpick inserted into the centre comes out clean. (Don't be concerned if cakes crack slightly in centres.)
7. Place on a rack, let cool for 5 minutes. With a blunt knife, loosen around the sides, remove the cakes and place on a rack. Let the cakes cool for 15 minutes. Using large palette knife, ease the cakes off the loose bottoms on to a rack. Let cool completely before icing.
8. To prepare the icing, use a double boiler. Place the first 7 ingredients in the top part and cook stirring over simmering water for 5 minutes. The mixture will be thick and smooth. Beat the egg yolks with a fork and blend. Pour in the carob mixture, stir and cook about 5 minutes until thick and smooth. Let cool. Remove the vanilla pod, pressing out the juices.
9. Place the fat in a large mixing bowl and beat on high speed until smooth. Beat in cooled carob mixture, a little at a time, until well blended. The icing will be thin. Chill about 30 minutes until spreadable.
10. To assemble, using serrated knife, slice each layer horizontally in half. Place bottom of one layer on sheet of greaseproof paper on a firm surface. Spread with one-fifth of the icing. Cover with a cake layer. Continue to ice between the layers, on top and around sides of the cake in an attractive pattern. Sprinkle the coconut around the outer edge of iced top layer. chill until icing is firm to the touch.
11. Write, using the almonds, 'Happy Birthday' in the centre of the cake, pressing each nut (not too forcefully) into the icing, or use a plastic decoration. Let stand at room temperature for 1 hour before serving.

SERVES: 16 or more

FUDGE ICING VARIATION: for a pourable consistency for serving over plain cake, desserts, ice cream or fruit, increase the evaporated milk to 300 ml/ 10 fl oz. Use 250 ml/ 8 fl oz in step 8. Stir in 30 ml/ 2 Tbsp unsalted butter/margarine blend at the end of step 8. Stir in as much of the remaining milk as necessary to thin to the desired consistency.

*TO CONVERT into an even more healthful recipe, use converted Batter and Cake Mix. For decoration around the edges of top layer, substitute chopped walnuts for the coconut , which is high in saturated fat.

3-JUICE GELS (K)

180 ml/ 6 fl oz unsweetened pineapple juice

180 ml/ 6 fl oz unsweetened dark grape juice

125 ml/ 4 fl oz unsweetened apple juice

15 ml/ 1 Tbsp sugar

7 g/ ¼ oz unflavoured gelatine

1. In a saucepan, bring the 3 juices to the boil, then stir in the sugar.
2. Place the gelatine in a medium bowl, add the hot fruit juices and stir until the gelatine is completely dissolved.
3. Pour into dessert dishes. Chill until set, then freeze.

SERVES 4

VARIATION: chill the mixture until it is the consistency of unbeaten egg whites. Stir in 125 ml/ 4 fl oz puréed fresh fruit or 180 g/ 10 oz chopped fresh fruit or whole berries. Chill until firm. Serves 6.

* PEACH ICE CREAM

350 ml/ 12 fl oz milk
125 ml/ 4 fl oz double cream
2.5 ml/ ½ tsp ground coriander
2.5 cm/ 1 inch length of vanilla
   pod, split
1 egg
30 ml/ 2 Tbsp sugar

5 ml/ 1 tsp cornflour dissolved in
   5 ml/ 1 tsp water
30 ml/ 2 Tbsp honey
3 ripe peaches, peeled and
   coarsely chopped

1. Bring the water in the bottom of a double boiler to the
   boil. Reduce the heat to simmering. In the top of the
   double boiler, combine and stir the milk, cream,
   coriander and vanilla pod. Cook until just below the
   boiling point. Remove from the heat.
2. Combine and blend the egg and sugar with a fork. Pour
   in a thin stream into the hot milk mixture, while
   constantly stirring. Place over simmering water and cook
   for 5 minutes, whisking from time to time.
3. Dribble in the cornflour mixture while whisking. Cook
   until the mixture coats the back of a spoon. Remove
   from the heat. Press out the juices from the vanilla pod
   and discard the bean. Let cool, whisking occasionally.
   Stir in the honey and peaches.
4. Pour into an ice cream maker, following the
   manufacturer's instructions, or pour into empty ice cube
   trays. Turn the refrigerator up to its coldest setting.
   Cover the tray and freeze, stirring from time to time.
   After 1 hour, vigorously stir with a wooden spoon.
   Return the tray to freezing compartment until mixture
   sets to desired consistency.

MAKES: about 500 ml/ 16 fl oz; serving size = 125 ml/ 4 fl oz

* **TO CONVERT** into an even more healthful recipe while
maintaining the flavour, reduce the fat by eliminating the
cream and increasing the milk to 500 ml/ 16 fl oz and
eliminating the sugar, increasing the honey to 45 ml/ 3
Tbsp and adding a pinch of ground cinnamon.

* BLACK CHERRY-BANANA ICE CREAM

350 ml/ 12 fl oz milk
125 ml/ 4 fl oz double cream
5 cm/ 2 inch length of vanilla
  pod, split
30 ml/ 2 Tbsp black cherry
  concentrate (available in
  health food shops)

30 ml/ 2 Tbsp Fruit Butter
  (page 112)
Dash of salt
2 egg yolks
1 ripe medium banana, mashed
15 ml/ 1 Tbsp honey

1. Bring the water in the bottom of a double boiler to the
   boil. Reduce the heat to simmering. In the top of the
   double boiler, combine and stir the first 6 ingredients
   and cook until just below the boiling point.
2. Lightly beat the egg yolks with a fork. Pour about 60 ml/
   2 fl oz hot liquid into a cup and blend. Pour the mixture
   back into the pan and cook for about 4 minutes until it
   coats the back of a wooden spoon. Stir in the banana.
   Press out the juices from the vanilla pod and discard the
   pod. Let cool, stirring occasionally. Stir in the honey.
3. Pour into an ice cream maker, following the
   manufacturer's instructions, or pour into empty ice cube
   trays. Turn the refrigerator up to its coldest setting.
   Cover the tray, and freeze, stirring from time to time.
   After 1 hour, vigorously stir with a wooden spoon.
   Return the tray to the freezing compartment until ice
   cream sets to desired consistency.

MAKES: about 500 ml/ 16 fl oz; serving size = 125 ml/ 4 fl oz

* TO CONVERT into an even more healthful recipe while
maintaining the flavour, eliminate the cream and increase
the milk to 500 ml/ 16 fl oz.

ICE CREAM MILK SHAKE (K)

250 ml/ 8 fl oz cold
  unsweetened apple juice

1 Scoop Peach or Black
  Cherry-Banana Ice Cream
  (page 141 or 142)

1. Combine the apple juice and ice cream in food processor
   or blender. Blend on high speed until smooth and
   frothy.
2. Pour into a tall glass and serve immediately.
SERVES: 1

ICED BANANA LOLLIES

4 ripe medium bananas
7.5 ml/ 1 ½ tsp unsalted
   butter/margarine blend
10 ml/ 2 tsp honey
60 ml/ 2 fl oz unsweetened
   apple juice
2.5 cm/1 inch piece vanilla pod,
   split
45 ml/ 3 Tbsp unsweetened
   carob powder

45 ml/ 3 Tbsp each unhulled
   sesame seeds, wheatgerm,
   and chopped walnuts
2.5 ml/ ½ tsp ground cinnamon
8 wooden lolly sticks

1. Place the unpeeled bananas in the freezing compartment for 20 minutes.
2. In small heavy-based saucepan, melt the butter/margarine blend over a low heat. While stirring, dribble in the honey. Add the apple juice and vanilla pod. Bring to the simmering point. Sprinkle in the carob, breaking up any lumps and stir until dissolved. Cook, uncovered about 3 minutes until mixture is satiny smooth and slightly thickened. Remove from the heat and let cool to room temperature.
3. Combine the sesame seeds, wheatgerm, nuts and cinnamon. Line a small baking tin with greaseproof paper. Sprinkle with half of the mixture.
4. Remove the bananas from the freezer and carefully peel. Cut the bananas in half. Insert wooden sticks into the bananas lengthways. Dip each into the carob mixture, gently rolling with a fork to coat. Lay on top of the wheatgerm mixture and sprinkle with the remaining wheatgerm mixture, turning with a fork to evenly coat.
5. Place in the freezing compartment. Lollies are ready to enjoy in 2 hours.

MAKES: 8 lollies

Recipes for the New 'Bright Cuisine'

These recipes are Bright Cuisine variants of healthy 'junk-food' recipes. You can also use them to plan your Bright Cuisine replacements in the Basic All-Family Menu Plan. The letter **K** means the recipe is simple enough for your kids to make under your supervision. Recipes are arranged under *Breakfast*, *Lunch* and *Dinner*.

Bright Cuisine Dishes for Breakfast

WHOLEMEAL BREAD

15 ml/ 1 Tbsp molasses
60 ml/ 2 fl oz warm water plus
   200 ml/ 7 fl oz water
10 ml/ 2 tsp dried yeast
300–480 g/10–14 oz plain flour
200 g/7 oz stoneground
   wholemeal flour
1.25 ml/ 1 tsp ground coriander

2.5 ml/ ½ tsp ground cinnamon
1.25 ml/ ¼ tsp salt
30 g/ 1 oz bran
30 ml/ 2 Tbsp skimmed dried
   milk
60 ml/ 2 fl oz low-fat plain
   yoghurt
15 ml/ 1 Tbsp oil
45 ml/ 3 Tbsp frozen apple juice
   concentrate

1. In a tall glass bowl, combine the molasses with 60 ml/ 2 fl oz warm water, stirring to dissolve. Sprinkle in the yeast and flour and stir. Let stand about 7 minutes until the mixture rises to top of the bowl.
2. Fit a food processor with a steel blade. Combine 330 g/ 11 oz plain flour, all the wholemeal flour, spices, salt, bran and dried milk and process on/off 4 times.
3. Add the yeast mixture and process until blended. Add the yoghurt and oil and process again for 10 seconds.
4. Combine and heat the apple juice concentrate and 200 ml/ 7 fl oz water until warm. With the food processor running, slowly pour the liquid through the feed tube and process until the dough rotates around the container 15 to 20 times, using the remaining flour if necessary, to make a non-sticky ball. Transfer to a work surface and knead by hand for 1 minute. Shape into a ball.

5. Lightly oil a large bowl. Drop the dough in, turning to coat. Cover with cling film and let rise at room temperature about 1 ½ hours until doubled in bulk. Knock back and knead briefly. Cut in half.
6. Shape each half into a ball. Flatten with hands. Using a rolling pin, roll each piece into a rectangle wide enough to fit a loaf tin. Tightly roll up, pinching the ends. Grease two 1 kg/ 2 lb tins and 2 sheets of greaseproof paper. Place dough seam down in the tins and cover with greaseproof paper. Let rise about 1 hour until well above the sides of tins. Pre-heat the oven to 190°C/375°F/Gas 5.
7. Bake for 35 to 40 minutes. Remove from the tin. Test for doneness by tapping bottom of loaves with knuckles. A hollow sound indicates the bread is done. If bread is not done, return the loaves to the oven and bake for another 5 minutes. Let cool completely before slicing.

MAKES: 2 loaves

VARIATION: Raisin Wholemeal Bread: add 45 g/ 1 ½ oz raisins to the saucepan in step 4 and heat until warm. Let the mixture cool for 10 minutes. Continue with the remainder of the instructions.

WHOLE MEAL POPOVERS (K)

2 large eggs
250 ml/ 8 fl oz milk
5 g/ 3 oz sifted plain flour
45 g/1 ½ oz sifted wholemeal flour
15 ml/1 Tbsp wheatgerm
1.25 ml/ ¼ tsp each salt and ground cinnamon
15 ml/ 1 Tbsp oil
Unsalted butter/margarine blend for ramekins

1. Pre-heat the oven to 200°C/400°F/Gas 6. Place the eggs and milk in a blender and blend on high speed for 5 seconds. Add the remaining ingredients except the fat and blend for 10 seconds. With a rubber spatula, scrape down the sides and bottom of the blender and blend about 20 seconds until smooth.
2. Grease six 150 ml/ 5 fl oz ramekins. Place on a baking tray. Half-fill each ramekin with batter. For well-baked brown crusted popovers, bake for 35 to 40 minutes. For light brown crusted popovers, reduce the heat to

375°F/190°C/Gas 5. Don't peek before prescribed time, or they'll all fall down.
3. Transfer to a rack and let cool for 3 minutes. With blunt knife, carefully circle each ramekin around sides to loosen. Remove popovers.

MAKES: 6 large popovers
SERVING SUGGESTION: serve with sugarless jam, or fill with scrambled eggs, or chicken, fish, meat or vegetables.

VARIATIONS: Spiced Popovers: add 1.25 ml/ ¼ tsp each ground ginger and coriander (or cardamom) to batter in step 1.
   Cheese Popovers: sprinkle each batter-filled ramekin with 5 ml/1 tsp freshly grated Parmesan or mozzarella cheese before baking.

NOTE: two simple yet crucial things to remember when preparing popovers: the oven must be *pre-heated* to exact prescribed temperature, and the batter must be beaten to smooth perfection.

FROZEN YOGHURT TUTTI-FRUTTI (K)

1 ripe banana
5 ml/ 1 tsp fresh lemon juice
45 ml/ 3 Tbsp unsalted smooth peanut butter
125 g/ 4 oz crushed unsweetened pineapple, drained

Pinch of ground cinnamon
2 pinches of ground allspice
350 ml/ 12 fl oz low-fat plain yoghurt
30 ml/ 2 Tbsp honey

1. Place the banana in a bowl. Mash with a fork, then sprinkle with lemon juice and mash again. Blend in the peanut butter, pineapple and spices.
2. Fold in the yoghurt. Dribble in the honey then fold in the remaining yoghurt.
3. Pour into an ice cream maker, following the manufacturer's instructions, or pour into empty ice cube trays. Turn the freezing compartment up to its coldest setting, cover the tray and freeze, stirring from time to time. After 1 hour, briskly beat. Return the tray to the freezer until mixture sets to desired consistency.

MAKES: about 500 ml/ 16 fl oz; serving size = 125 ml/ 4 fl oz

Bright Cuisine Dishes for Lunch

BROCCOLI BRISQUE

30 ml/ 2 Tbsp corn oil
125 g/4 oz shallots, very finely chopped, or combination chopped shallots and onions
1 large bunch fresh broccoli florets
15 ml/ 1 Tbsp cider vinegar
600 ml/ 20 fl oz 'Canned' Chicken Stock (page 112) or stock made with low-sodium vegetable seasoning
125 ml/ 4 fl oz unsweetened apple juice

15 ml/ 1 Tbsp cornflour
15 ml/ 1 Tbsp mild curry powder
2.5 ml/ ½ tsp freshly grated nutmeg
1.25 ml/ ¼ tsp salt
Several sprigs of fresh parsley tied into a bundle
45 ml/ 3 Tbsp evaporated skimmed milk or ordinary skimmed milk
30 ml/ 2 Tbsp grated carrot

1. Heat the oil in a heavy-based large saucepan until hot Sauté the shallots until wilted but not brown, stirring often. Add the broccoli and sauté for 1 minute, then add vinegar and cook for 1 minute. Then add the stock and apple juice and bring to a boil.
2. Dissolve the cornflour in a little of the liquid; stir in with the curry, half of nutmeg, and the salt. Drop in the parsley bundle. Reduce the heat to simmering. Cover and simmer for 12 minutes, stirring once. Uncover and cool. Discard parsley bundle.
3. Pour the mixture into a blender, half at a time. Add the remaining 1.25 ml/ ¼ tsp nutmeg and purée until smooth.
   Return to the saucepan and beat in the milk. Re-heat to just under boiling point, then pour into serving dishes, sprinkle with carrot, and serve.

SERVES: 5

147

TOFU CASSEROLE— it's a Whole Meal!

500 g/ 1 lb aubergine, scrubbed and cut into 1 cm/ ½ inch slices

30 ml/ 2 Tbsp each corn and Italian olive oil, combined

2 tofu cakes (about 350 g/ ¾ lb)

150 g/ 5 oz chopped onions or combination of shallots and onion

30 ml/ 2 Tbsp finely chopped garlic

75 g/ 2 ½ oz green pepper, coarsely chopped

125 g/ 4 oz button mushrooms, trimmed, rinsed, dried and thinly sliced

1.25 ml/ ¼ tsp salt (optional)

2.5 ml/ ½ tsp each dried marjoram and thyme leaves, crushed, and ground ginger

60 ml/ 2 fl oz 'Canned' Chicken Stock (page 112) or stock made with low-sodium vegetable seasoning

375 g/ 12 oz canned tomatoes, crushed

30 ml/ 2 Tbsp unsweetened apple juice

30 ml/ 2 Tbsp finely chopped fresh parsley

75 g/ 3 oz mozzarella cheese, grated

Freshly ground black pepper (optional)

1. Arrange the aubergine slices on a baking tray and brush each side with 30 ml/2 Tbsp oil. Grill until lightly browned on each side, then remove from the grill and set aside.
2. Cut the tofu into 1 cm/ ½ inch slices. Lay on double sheets of kitchen paper and blot with another sheet of paper. Let drain.
3. Heat the 30 ml/ 2 tbsp oil over medium heat in a non-stick frying pan. Sauté the onions, garlic, green pepper and mushrooms until softened. Combine the salt, marjoram, thyme and ginger. Sprinkle over the mixture and sauté for 1 minute. Add the stock and cook for 1 minute, then mix in tomatoes, apple juice and parsley. Bring to simmering point and simmer, uncovered, for 3 to 5 minutes, or until mixture is thick and most of liquid is reduced.
4. Pre-heat the oven to 190°C/375°F/Gas 3. Assemble the casserole in alternate layers of aubergine, tofu, tomato mixture and cheese. Bake, uncovered, until lightly browned, 40 to 45 minutes. Sprinkle with freshly ground black pepper, if desired.

SERVES: 4 to 5

CHINESE-STYLE SAUTÉED PRAWNS

45 ml/ 3 Tbsp cornflour
2.5 ml/ ½ tsp ground ginger, dry mustard and dried basil leaves, crushed
1.25 ml/ ¼ tsp dried thyme
Pinch each of salt and cayenne pepper
5 ml/ 1 tsp finely chopped lemon rind

600 g/ 1 ¼ lb medium raw prawns, peeled and deveined
15 ml/ 1 Tbsp fresh lemon juice, plus juice from ½ lemon
30 ml/ 2 Tbsp peanut oil
45 ml/ 3 Tbsp finely chopped shallot
2.5 ml/ ½ tsp finely chopped garlic
5 ml/ 1 tsp reduced-sodium soy sauce

1. Prepare a light coating by combining the cornflour, seasonings and lemon rind in a bowl and blending well. Set aside.
2. Dry the prawns. Sprinkle with 15 ml/ 1 tbsp lemon juice, turning to evenly coat. Let stand at room temperature for 30 minutes.
3. Pat lightly with kitchen towels. Add all the prawns to the bowl with the coating and, using your hands, toss and turn until the prawns are lightly coated.
4. Heat the oil in large non-stick frying pan. Spread the shallot and garlic evenly across the pan and sauté over medium-high heat for 1 minute. Lay the prawns on top of the mixture and sauté on each side until lightly browned, about 8 minutes total cooking time.
5. Sprinkle with soy sauce and the juice of ½ lemon. Turn and sauté for 1 minute. Serve hot.

SERVES: 4

149

PEANUT BUTTER MILK SHAKE (K)

3 ice cubes, crushed
125 ml/ 4 fl oz skimmed milk
60 ml/ 2 fl oz unsweetened
  pineapple juice
15 ml/ 1 Tbsp unsalted peanut
  butter

1 ripe or small banana or 125 g/
  4 oz fresh berries in season
5 ml/ 1 tsp honey (optional)

Place all ingredients in a blender or food processor. Blend on
high speed for 1 minute. Serve at once.

SERVES: 1
VARIATION: the addition of a pinch of ground ginger,
cinnamon or cardamom or any combination is a flavour
booster (for fruit milk shakes, too).

COFFEE ICE CREAM

250 ml/ 8 fl oz milk
180 ml/ 6 fl oz evaporated
  skimmed milk
2.5 cm/ 1 inch piece vanilla pod,
  split
1.25 ml/ ½ tsp ground cinnamon
Pinch of ground allspice

30 ml/ 2 Tbsp instant coffee
Pinch of salt
2 egg yolks
30 ml/ 2 Tbsp honey

1. Bring some water in the bottom of a double boiler to the
   boil. Reduce the heat to simmering. In the top of the
   double boiler, combine and stir all the ingredients,
   except the egg yolk and honey. Cool for 5 minutes,
   stirring often.
2. Lightly beat egg yolks with a fork. Pour about 60 ml/ 2 fl
   oz hot liquid into a cup and blend. Pour the mixture
   back into the pan and cook about 4 minutes until it coats
   back of a spoon. Remove from the heat. Press out the
   juices from the vanilla pod, then discard. Cool, whisking
   occasionally, then stir in honey.
3. Pour into an ice cream maker, following the
   manufacturer's instructions, or pour into empty ice cube
   trays. Turn the refrigerator up to its coldest setting.
   Cover tray and freeze, stirring from time to time. After 1
   hour, briskly whisk. Return the tray to the freezing
   compartment until ice cream sets to desired consistency.

MAKES: about 500 ml/16 fl oz; serving size = 125 ml/ 4 fl oz

Bright Cuisine Dishes for Dinner

NEW-FASHIONED MUSHROOM AND BARLEY SOUP

15 g/ ½ oz dried mushrooms, preferably a dark variety
300ml/ 10 fl oz water
250 g/ 8 oz lean stewing beef cut into 1 cm/ ½ inch pieces
15 ml/ 3 tsp Spicy Mix (page 111)
30 ml/ 2 Tbsp Italian olive or corn oil
250 ml/ 8 oz Frozen Vegetable Mix (page 109)

20 ml/ 4 tsp balsamic vinegar
750 ml/ 24 fl oz 'Canned' Chicken Stock (page 112) or stock made with low-sodium vegetable seasoning
5 ml/ 1 tsp low-sodium vegetable seasoning
30 ml/ 2 Tbsp tomato paste
60 g/ 2 oz pot barley, rinsed

1. Rinse the mushrooms, then break into small pieces. Place in cup with 60 ml/ 2 fl oz water and soak for 30 minutes.
2. Sprinkle meat with 7.5 ml/ 1 ½ tsp Spicy Mix, working well into the meat. Heat the oil in a large heavy-based saucepan. Add the meat and quickly sear, stirring and cooking for 1 minute. Reduce the heat to moderate then add the Vegetable Mix, stir and cook about 3 minutes until vegetables begin to soften.
3. Stir in the vinegar and cook for 1 minute. Add the remaining water and ingredients, and the mushrooms with their soaking liquid. Bring to the boil, reduce the heat to simmering, cover and cook for 1 ½ hours, stirring from time to time. Remove from heat and let stand for 10 minutes, covered, before serving.

SERVES: 5

POACHED CHICKEN WITH CREAMY SAUCE

Chicken:

4 chicken breast fillets, skinned
1 small celery stalk, coarsely
  chopped
1 small onion, coarsely chopped
30 ml/ 2 Tbsp grated carrot

2 sprigs of fresh parsley and 1
  bay leaf tied together
350 ml/ 12 fl oz 'Canned'
  Chicken Stock (page 112) or
  stock made with low-sodium
  vegetable seasoning
Watercress sprigs for garnish

Creamy Sauce:

10 ml/ 2 tsp unsalted
  butter/margarine blend
15 ml/ 1 Tbsp finely chopped
  shallot
20 ml/ 4 tsp plain flour
125–180 ml/ 4–6 fl oz poaching
  liquid
2.5 ml/ ½ tsp each dried sage
  leaves and mild curry powder

45 ml/ 3 Tbsp evaporated
  skimmed milk
30 ml/ 2 Tbsp freshly grated
  Parmesan cheese
15 ml/ 1 Tbsp chopped fresh
  parsley
Pinch of salt
Cayenne pepper, to taste
1.25–1.5 ml/ ¼–½ tsp fresh
  lemon juice

1. Wash and dry the chicken thoroughly. Place in wide pan or a non-stick frying pan large enough to hold the pieces in one layer. Strew with the vegetables and drop in the parsley bundle. Add enough stock to barely cover. Bring to the boil, reduce the heat to simmer, cover and simmer for 20 minutes, basting with the stock twice at equal intervals.

2. Transfer the chicken to a hot plate. Cover to keep warm. Strain 180 ml/ 6 fl oz cooking liquid into a measuring cup, reserving the remaining stock for another dish.

3. Melt the butter/margarine blend in a heavy-based small saucepan (preferable enamelled) until melted. Add the shallot and sauté without browning for 1 minute. Stir in the flour with a wooden spoon and cook over low heat for 1 minute. Whisk in 125 ml/ 4 fl oz cooking liquid. Cook until thickened, then sprinkle in the sage and curry powder. Whisk and cook over low heat for 1 minute.

4. Add the milk and parsley. Cook and stir with a whisk for 2 minutes. Pour any juices that have drained from chicken into sauce, using the remaining stock to thin down the sauce to the desired consistency.

5. Sprinkle with salt, cayenne pepper and 1.25 ml/ ½ tsp

lemon juice, whisking to blend. Cook for 30 seconds. Taste and add more cayenne and/or lemon juice if desired. Pour over the chicken, garnish with watercress and serve at once.

SERVES: 4; Creamy Sauce: 210 ml/7 fl oz

CHICKEN WITH APPLES

30 ml/ 2 Tbsp oil
180 g/ 6 oz Frozen
 Vegetable Mix (page 109)
30 g/ 1 oz fresh mushrooms,
 trimmed, rinsed, dried and
 coarsely chopped
1.5 kg/ 3 lb chicken, skinned,
 wings removed and cut into
 eights
30 ml/ 2 Tbsp Spicy Mix
 (page 111)

15 ml/ 1 Tbsp apple cider
 vinegar
15 ml/1 Tbsp tomato paste
15 ml/ 1 Tbsp reduced-sodium
 soy sauce
125 ml/ 4 fl oz each tomato
 juice, preferably low-sodium,
 and apple juice
Pinch of salt
2 Golden Delicious apples,
 cored, peeled and sliced

1. Heat the oil in a well-seasoned cast-iron frying pan or flameproof casserole until hot. Add the Vegetable Mix and mushrooms and cook, stirring about 5 minutes until softened. Spread the mixture over the pan.
2. Sprinkle and rub the chicken with the Spicy Mix. Lay on top of the the sautéed mixture in one layer and cook for 5 minutes over medium-high heat without turning. Turn, then cook for 5 minutes more.
3. Pour the vinegar around the sides of the pan and cook for 1 minute.
4. Combine and blend the tomato paste, soy sauce, tomato juice and apple juice. Pour around the sides of the pan and sprinkle with salt (omit if regular tomato juice is used). Bring to the boil, then stir the sauce and turn the chicken parts to coat. Reduce the heat to simmering and cover and simmer for 65 minutes, turning twice.
5. Add the apples, pushing them into the sauce. Re-cover and cook for 15 minutes.
6. Transfer the chicken to large serving plate with slotted spoon. Cover to keep warm. Place the pan over medium-high heat and reduce the sauce, stirring about 4 minutes until thickened. Spoon the sauce and apples over chicken and serve at once.

SERVES: 4

CHOC-O-CHIP ICE MILK

125 ml/ 4 fl oz skimmed milk
300 ml/ 10 fl oz evaporated
  skimmed milk
75 g/ 1 ½ oz unsweetened
  carob chips
30 ml/ 2 Tbsp instant coffee

2.5 cm/ 1 inch piece vanilla pod,
  split
1.25 ml/ ¼ tsp ground
  cinnamon
45 ml/ 2 Tbsp honey

1. Bring some water in the bottom of a double boiler to the boil. Reduce the heat to simmering. Combine and stir the skimmed milk, 60 ml/ 2 fl oz evaporated skimmed milk, 60 g/ 2 oz carob chips, coffee, vanilla and cinnamon in the top part. Cook until the chips are almost melted. Remove from the heat and stir in the remaining chips. Let cool, stirring occasionally. Press out the juices from the vanilla pod and discard.
2. Add the honey and blend, then stir in the remaining evaporated milk.
3. Pour into an ice cream maker, following the manufacturer's instructions, or pour into empty ice cube trays. Turn the refrigerator up to its coldest setting. Cover tray and freeze, stirring from time to time. After 1 hour, briskly whisk. Return to the freezing compartment until the ice cream sets to desired consistency.

Makes: about 600 ml/ 15 fl oz; serving size = 125 ml/ 4 fl oz

RECOMMENDED READING

ABC of Nutrition, A Stewart Truswell, British Medical Association, 1986

The Amino Revolution, Robert Erdmann, Century, 1987

Attitudes towards the feeding and nutrition of young children: first report on a Health Education Council Project concerned with the formation of eating habits and attitudes towards food within the family, Nickie Charles and Marion Kerr, HEC, 1985

The Amazing Brain, Robert Ornstein and Richard F Thompson, Chatto, 1985

The Biology of Human Foetal Growth, D F Roberts and A M Thomson, eds, Taylor and Francis, 1976

Children Need Food, Harry Undy, Wayland, 1987

Cooking for a Baby, Sylvia Hull, Penguin Books, 1979

Coping Successfully with your Hyperactive Child, Paul Carson, Sheldon, 1987

Diet and Disease, E Cheraskin, W M Ringsdorf and J W Clark, Keats Publishing, 1977

Diet, Nutrition and Health: Report of the Board of Science and Education, BMA, 1986

The Diets of British Schoolchildren, R W Wenlock, M M Disselduff, R K Skinner, DHSS, 1986

Dr Spock's Baby and Child Care, Benjamin Spock and Michael B Rothanberg, Bantam, 1985

The Everyman Companion to Food and Nutrition, Sheila Bingham, Dent, 1987

Feeding Your Family, Miriam Stoppard, Viking, 1987

Get Ready to Feed Your New Baby, Jane Howarth, Book Guild, 1985

Growing up with Good Food, Catherine Lewis, ed, Unwin, 1982

Hypoglycaemia in Infancy, Albert Aynsley-Green and Gyula Soltesz, Churchill Llivingstone, 1985

Infant Feeding and Family Nutrition, Sally Parsonage and June Clark, John Wiley, 1981

Is Your Child Allergic?: a guide for parents, Jan A Kuzembo, Thorsons, 1988

Manual of Nutrition, MAFF 9th edition, HMSO, 1985

Neuronal Man: The Biology of Mind, Jean-Pierre Changeux, Oxford University Press, 1986

Nutrients, Mental and Elemental, Carl Pfeiffer, Keats, 1975

Nutri-score: Rate Yourself Plan for Better Nutrition, Ruth Fremes and Zak Sabry, Eyre Methuen, 1977

Nutrition Against Disease, Roger S. Williams, Bantam, 1981

Nutrition and Development, Margaret Biswas and Per Pinstrup-Andersen, eds, Oxford University Press, 1985

Nutrition for Children, Dorothy E Francis, Blackwell, 1986

Nutrition in Pregnancy and Early Childhood: the proceedings of a symposium organised by the Institute of Obstetrics and Gynaecology (University of London) and the Coronary Prevention Group, Coronary Prevention Group, 1986

The Parent's Nutrition Book, Margaret McWilliams, John Wiley, 1986

Present Day Practice in Infant Feeding: Third Report, HMSO, 1988

Understanding Allergies, Mary Steel, Which? Books, 1986

INDEX

RECIPE INDEX

* before title = recipe can be converted to an even more healthy one using the notes at the end of the recipe, (K) after title = simple enough for kids to make under supervision